RUS · RA

A · SERBIA · EG

ORDAN · LEB

ENIA · TURKEY

INE · GREEC

OMANIA · SLO

A · EGYPT · SYR

Nistisima

Mum and Dad,

Thank you for everything you do for us.
There is no way I could have written this book
(or written or cooked anything, for that matter)
without your constant love and support.

x

Nistisima

The secret to delicious vegan cooking from the Mediterranean and beyond

Georgina
Hayden

BLOOMSBURY PUBLISHING
LONDON • OXFORD • NEW YORK • NEW DELHI • SYDNEY

BLOOMSBURY PUBLISHING
Bloomsbury Publishing Plc
50 Bedford Square, London WC1B 3DP, UK
29 Earlsfort Terrace, Dublin 2, Ireland

First published in Great Britain 2022

A catalogue record for this book is available from the British Library.

ISBN: HB: 978-1-5266-3068-1; e-book: 978-1-5266-3069-8

2 4 6 8 10 9 7 5 3

Project Editor: Holly O'Neill
Designer: Anna Green at Siulen Design
Photographer: Kristin Perers
Food Stylist: Joss Herd
Prop Stylist: Tabitha Hawkins
Indexer: Vanessa Bird

Printed and bound in China by C&C Offset Printing Co. Ltd

FSC www.fsc.org MIX Paper from responsible sources FSC® C008047

To find out more about our authors and books visit www.bloomsbury.com and sign up for our newsletters.

Eat to live, not live to eat

SOCRATES
(469–399 BCE)

Contents

Introduction

The idea to write *Nistisima* began while I was researching *Taverna*, my previous book which is centred around Cyprus, my family and all of our inherited recipes. When I was recording the stories I'd been told, the recipes that were shared, the foods I have been brought up eating, I realised how many of them revolve around the Greek Orthodox calendar. How we ate was especially governed by the days and weeks during the year with fasting rules: no dairy, no meat or fish on certain days; no olive oil or wine on others. Growing up, I never questioned why we have countless cake recipes that are oil-based and contain no eggs, or that we drank almond 'milk', long before it became trendy in café culture, but now I understand that this came about from necessity.

The Greek word *nistisima* translates as Lenten, or fasting, foods. These are foods that, on the whole, do not contain any animal products and adhere to the Orthodox church's fasting rules. It is the plant-based recipes and traditions that I am exploring in this book. Those of Orthodox faith can spend up to 200 days a year 'fasting' or eating in this restricted way, and historically our recipes and diets in Greece and Cyprus reflect this (despite the kebabs and grills that you may be familiar with). It is so ingrained in our everyday life that it isn't uncommon to find sections of the local bakery or deli dedicated to plant-based foods. While there isn't a huge appreciation for veganism, or even vegetarianism, in Cyprus, if you were to explain your diet as '*nistisimo*' people would know exactly what you meant.

It is important to note that this is not a religious or diet book. I am not here to tell you how to pray, how to live your life or even how to eat – this book is for everyone. Perhaps you happen to be Orthodox and are looking for recipes to try while fasting, or maybe you are adopting a plant-based diet and need inspiration for meals. It could be that you see the recipes and stories of your relatives here, your roots, and you want to feel that connection with home. Or you simply want to eat more vegetables. Why and how you use this book is up to you.

Fasting is a historic practice among many communities and religions, each with their own rules, whether it is cutting out certain food groups, or not eating at certain times. And, as well as religion, there is nothing new about abstaining from or eliminating certain foods. It is said that fasting has been used therapeutically since at least the year 5BCE, when Hippocrates prescribed to some patients that they abstain from food and drink. And of course, fasting has come under the spotlight in recent years, as diets such as intermittent fasting have risen dramatically in popularity. So in a time when many of us are now looking at our own diets and ways to change our eating (whether it be for health, the environment or frugality), these recipes and traditions feel more relevant than ever.

Why

The purpose of fasting for Lent is to 'give something up' as a form of self-discipline, to be able to reflect and prepare before a large religious celebration. By observing forty days of Lent those of Christian faith aim to replicate Jesus's withdrawal into the wilderness. For others, whether of faith or not, abstinence and fasting can be purely a way of cutting back, taking stock and reassessing.

The quote at the beginning of the introduction is attributed to the Greek philosopher Socrates (coincidentally, my maiden-namesake): eat to live, not live to eat. I used to shudder at the thought of being someone who ate to live, rather than lived to eat. I was interpreting his quote on a basic level, describing a person who purely ate to function. However, I believe Socrates meant something deeper: food should be nourishing; energy to power our lives. Something I noticed from recipe-testing this book is that the recipes are full of flavour and (as you'll see I often note) quietly addictive, but I never felt sluggish after eating and the desire to over-indulge just wasn't there. I'm not trying to sell you on veganism, and meat still has a place in my kitchen and on my table; however, a prolonged period of eating this way did leave me feeling 'lighter', for want of a better word.

Depending on where you are reading this, the likelihood is you live in a society where almost all foods are readily available to you, at all times. We never have to wait any more, food can be eaten on the go and before we ever feel truly hungry. The idea of taking time for a meal really resonates with me, and is relevant to the foods, stories and recipes in this book. The monks of Mount Athos only eat twice a day, but they sit down and take their time. Even in times of fasting, it's important to eat well.

When my family gets together to eat, no one is presented with a plate of food that's already been portioned. Usually, we sit down at a table laden with many dishes. What could be considered the 'main' dish will be laid on the table in its cooking vessel, and alongside that will be a salad, some dips, a few preserves and bread. It looks like a lot of food but it's about the ritual of sitting together, talking, slowly grazing and appreciating what is in front of you. I really believe that the longer you take to eat, the more your brain acknowledges what has been consumed, the less likely you are to feel hungry again just hours later. And even during times where we aren't fasting, Mediterranean food is rarely too heavy or rich. Yes, there are slow-cooked meats and grills. But historically these were only eaten once a week – meat was and still is (compared to vegetables and grains) expensive. A few slices of cheese as part of a meal based around vegetables is far more common. All of this, alongside the fact that the Mediterranean diet is still labelled one of the healthiest in the world, is worth taking note of if we are to look at our own eating habits.

Beyond Greece and Cyprus...

Growing up with yiayias (grandmothers) who often fasted, I was familiar with all the obvious *nistisimo* foods. But as I delved into research for this book and spoke to family and friends who adhere to the fasting rules, they all had recipes and tales I hadn't heard before. The soup that was supposedly eaten by Jesus before he died; the biscuits that are eaten to break the Christmas fast; the soup the monks make on Mount Athos. The more people I talked to and questions I asked, the more I heard about other countries' fasting foods – as of course the Orthodox faith is practised worldwide. There are Coptic Christians in Egypt who fast for 210 days a year, as do Maronites in Lebanon and Syria, and the Orthodox community in Russia and much of Eastern Europe. There is an Orthodox church in Kerala whose fasts are filled with fragrant, spiced foods. Each community and country has their own traditions and I have attempted to include a range of recipes.

The foods from all around the eastern Mediterranean and Middle East feel similar, familiar, but I have tried to celebrate the differences between country and place. What is called *fakes* in Greece (green lentils cooked with rice) is called *faki moutzentra* in Cyprus, which is more influenced by the Lebanese and Middle Eastern version of the same dish, *mujadara*. It becomes richer, embellished along the way. To untangle the origins of certain dishes which appear throughout the Middle East and eastern

Mediterranean (and the Balkans, too) is often an impossible task. The recipes have travelled along with people and empires, the stories have changed – and that is the beauty of these foods.

I have been lucky to talk to some wonderful people as part of my research, from my neighbour and Cypriot deli owner Erene Panteli, whose family are strict fasters, to Sharice Babakhani, whose Armenian grandmother, Azadouhi, fasted most of her life. Sharice was kind enough to not only pass on her grandmother's recipes, but to send me videos of her making them. Watching Azadouhi kneading red lentil kofte (page 194) was as calming to watch as it is to recreate. Her recipes and stories travel far and wide, starting in Turkey where she was born, before fleeing the Armenian genocide in the early 20th century, relocating to Cyprus then to the UK.

Russian food writer Alissa Timoshkina had similar stories to my own of fasting. How archetypal Russian men willingly put down their grills for lighter, more wholesome meals during Lent, and how restaurants and cafés that may not usually offer vegetarian alternatives adapt their menus to offer plant-based Orthodox suitable meals during Lent. Ukrainian food writer Olia Hercules says the same of Ukraine, but explained she didn't have a strong connection to or experience of fasting, which was probably due to the *Holodomor*, the horrific famine that killed millions of Ukrainians in the early 1930s. Because of this, she told me, to actively cut out food was unthinkable. Olia kindly translated literature written by Russian and Ukrainian priests on the foods and drinks they consumed. She told me how ferments such as kvass (page 275) are made prior to times of fasting, in order to sustain worshippers alongside simple meals. This is not something we do a lot in Cyprus, so I found it fascinating and have adopted it into my own fasting rituals.

Mount Athos

As well as my heritage, one of the other reasons for the Greek base and geographical spread of recipes in this book is due to Mount Athos. Positioned in north-eastern Greece, Mount Athos is an important and prominent centre for the Eastern Orthodox church. Dating back to at least 800CE, today it hosts twenty monasteries and more than 2,000 monks not only from Greece, but a range of Eastern Orthodox countries including Romania, Georgia, Macedonia, Serbia and Russia. The monks live an ascetic and isolated life as, despite being connected to mainland Greece, Mount Athos is only accessible by boat. Those who want to visit need to obtain a visa first and, unfortunately for my research, only men are allowed on the mountain (the only females on Mount Athos are the cats).

The monks are mostly self-sufficient, growing and making almost everything they need. Food and cooking make up a large part of the daily rituals on the mountain, and each monastery has a dedicated cook or team of cooks to feed the monks. For this book, Father Theonas from Vatopedi monastery graciously answered my questions about their days and diets. Father Epiphanios, who sadly died while I was writing this book, is the most famous monk in terms of cooking, and wrote a wonderful book all about their diets and traditions, with more than 100 fasting-friendly recipes (titled *The Cuisine of the Holy Mountain Athos*). He believed that the key to flavoursome Lenten food is time – at the end of the day you are not using richly flavoured animal fats, so that depth of flavour has to come from careful cooking. If you are adopting a vegan or plant-based diet this is one of the key messages.

'I learned close to the Elders how to fry an onion over a low heat, because, as they would say, the slow and more delicate an onion is, as fried it turns golden brown, the more delicious the meal will be. I learned that at the end of the cooking process, all meals require patience and perseverance, when over a charcoal fire we wait for the remaining liquids of the food to be absorbed.'
Father Epiphanios, *The Cuisine of the Holy Mountain Athos*

An alternative 'why'

For some, the reason to fast is more emotional than religious. Those of us living far away from our home, or the country we are rooted to, will manifest that connection through food. The smells, tactile reward of handling ingredients, sitting and eating with others – nothing evokes such strong memories. I've often wondered whether immigrants embrace traditional elements of their culture with more enthusiasm than if they were in their homelands. When my husband and I planned our wedding, there were elements of the celebration that I wanted to include that those living in Cyprus no longer adhere to, but my yearning to connect to my roots spurred me on to adopt them. The emotions that go with cooking, eating and a sense of belonging run so deep and are so entwined that I've found even those who aren't otherwise devout will fast or observe the traditions in some way, as a connection to home and people.

The rules: fasts of the year

For me, fasting isn't a fad or crash diet, and this book isn't a guide for that. Fasting is part of my cultural and spiritual world, and the rules of fasting give the book – and I suppose my life – context.

FAST DAYS AND EXCEPTIONS

In the Orthodox liturgical calendar every Wednesday and Friday are fast days, excluding ones that fall in the weeks below:

- The week between the Sunday of the Publican and the Pharisee (in spring, before Easter Lent) and the Sunday of the Prodigal Son (two weeks later): all foods may be eaten
- The week before Cheesefare (or Forgiveness) Sunday: dairy, eggs and fish may be eaten; it is only meat that is abstained from
- The week following Easter Sunday (Bright Week): all foods may be eaten
- The week following the Sunday of Pentecost: all foods may be eaten
- The days between Christmas and Epiphany: all foods may be eaten, except for on 5th January which is a strict fast day

The large fasting periods are as follows:

- **The Fast of Lent/the Great Fast**
  These are days leading up to and including Holy Week, from Clean Monday to Holy Saturday before Easter Sunday. Fish is allowed on 25th March (Annunciation Day) and on Palm Sunday.
- **The Fast of the Holy Apostles**
  This runs from All Saints' Day up until the evening of the Feast of Saint Peter and Saint Paul on 28th June. Fish is allowed during this fast, except on Wednesdays and Fridays.
- **The Fast for the Assumption of the Virgin Mary**
  This starts on 1st August and runs until 14th August. Fish is allowed on 6th August for the Feast of the Transfiguration.
- **The Christmas Fast**
  Like Easter Lent, this fast lasts forty days, starting on 15th November and running until 24th December. However, due to various saint days during this period there are days when feasting is allowed. Fish can be eaten up until 17th December, except on Wednesdays and Fridays.

There are special days of strict fasts, where we do not eat meat, dairy, fish or oil, or drink wine. If these days fall on a Saturday or Sunday then oil and wine are allowed (the only Saturday of the year on which we do not eat oil or drink wine is Holy Saturday):

- 5th January – the day before Epiphany
- 29th August – the Feast of Beheading of St John the Forerunner (John the Baptist)
- 14th September – the Feast of the Elevation of the Holy Cross
- 24th December – the day before Christmas

There are feasts on which fish can be eaten on a Wednesday and Friday:

- 7th January – the Synaxis of St John the Forerunner
- 2nd February – the Presentation of the Lord
- 24th June – the Birth of the Forerunner
- 29th June – St Peter and St Paul's Day
- 6th August – the Transfiguration of the Lord
- 15th August – the Repose of the Theotokos ('God-bearer', Mary, mother of Jesus)
- 8th September – the Nativity of the Theotokos
- 14th November – St Philip's Day
- 21st November – the Entrance of the Theotokos

KATHARA DEFTERA AND OTHER SYMBOLIC DAYS

While even secular people in the West are familiar with Good Friday and Shrove Tuesday (who doesn't love Pancake Day?), we have many other symbolic days and times in the Orthodox faith and in Eastern Christianity. First is *Apókries*, the carnival season that lasts the three weeks and four Sundays before Lent (it finishes on the Sunday before Clean Monday). It is a time to eat meat and dairy and drink wine, but also a chance to start thinking about slowly weaning off these foods (the word carnival comes from the Latin *carnem levare* which means 'without meat'). It is marked with celebrations, music and dance; in carnivals throughout Greece and Cyprus people adopt fancy dress and masks. The processions and feasting all come from ancient ceremonies that honour Dionysus, the Greek god of wine, fertility and divine intoxication. If you can ever time a trip to Greece during this period, do so – it is huge amounts of fun, especially the last weekend where the celebrations start on the Thursday preceding Clean Monday. There are towns and cities known for their festivities – Patras and Xanthi are the most famous.

The Thursday before Lent is called *Tsiknopempti*, which translates as 'smoky Thursday'. This is due to the smell of the barbecues that fill the streets; it is one of the last opportunities to eat meat for almost five weeks, and people take the responsibility very seriously. The carnivals continue until the Sunday, also known as *Tyrofagos* – Cheesefare Sunday. A festival day a bit like Tsiknopempti, this is the last day to eat dairy, and traditionally only dairy products are eaten on this day.

Kathara Deftera, meaning Clean Monday, marks the first day of Lent. In Greece and Cyprus it is a public holiday, and *nistisimo* food is cooked, including a bread called *lagana* that is only made on this day (see page 29), and shellfish is eaten in abundance. It is also marked by flying kites, a symbol of being closer to the divine.

These days of fasts and feasts will, more often than not, fall differently to those of the Catholic and other Christian churches. This is because the Orthodox church calculates the date for Easter using the Julian calendar, whereas other churches use the Gregorian calendar.

EATING SEAFOOD, OLIVE OIL AND OTHER RULES

For the sake of accessibility, I decided to make this book strictly plant-based, as this is the main basis of *nistisimo* food. However, at home, I sometimes eat seafood as there are rules within Orthodox fasting that mean you are able to eat shellfish some days. It's also worth noting that on most fasting weekdays you aren't allowed to eat olive oil.

Seafood

The rule is that seafood with a backbone or seafood that bleeds is mostly prohibited during times of fasting. So, shellfish, octopus and *tarama* (fish roe) are allowed. To keep things easy, I have left these recipes out; however, if you are adhering to the Orthodox rules (as opposed to following a vegetarian or vegan diet), here are some simple suggestions for the kind of seafood I might have with vegetable dishes.

- Barbecued or pickled octopus – you can either make your own or you can buy jars of good-quality pickled octopus. (There is a list of suppliers on page 290.)
- Garithes saganaki – Greek fried prawns with tomato and feta
- Mussels
- Prawns in lemon and pepper

- Taramasalata – making your own is great but you can pick up good quality ready-made tubs. If you are not vegan, a dish of taramasalata as part of a meal (with pita and olives) is wonderful.

There are also some days when you are allowed to eat all kinds of seafood. If you're not bound by any restrictions, a side of simply grilled sea bass or mackerel, for example, would be perfect with many of the vegetable and grain dishes in this book.

Olive oil

Olive oil is banned during the fasting weeks, apart from on specific days (see previous pages) and weekends. While it is not an animal product, this rule reflects an ancient tradition of storing olive oil in sheep's skin. Many people use vegetable or sunflower oil instead; however, you will find some that won't use any oil in their cooking. The choice is yours. Most of my recipes use oil, but feel free to mix it up. If you want to adhere to the strict fasting rules of no oil there are plenty of dishes where you can leave it out, and simply use water to steam and soften vegetables.

Honey

I wouldn't normally think to mention honey, as it is not considered a fasting food in the Orthodox church. I appreciate there will be people who read this book that adhere to a vegan diet and for whom honey is a no-go. In respect of that, I have offered alternatives where it is used in a recipe. However, I also want to be respectful of the cuisine, foods and traditions I am writing about, and to leave it out just would not be right – honey production is a large part of Greek agriculture and a source of pride. Most of the time it can be switched with a sweet alternative like agave or maple syrup, or even regular sugar would be fine.

Dairy and dairy-free products

Dairy is traditionally not eaten on strict fast days; however, for various reasons people may still want or need to include dairy in their diet. It's an easy ingredient to add to the recipes in this book. We once had a home visit from our local priest – he was performing an exorcism on the house (another story for another time – it's a good one!) and it was during the Easter period. His wife attended also, and when offered a cup of tea with soy milk, she asked for regular milk. They were an older couple, and even though she was a priest's wife she couldn't quite cut out dairy. Fair enough, I say. So while I have kept the recipes plant-based, I have occasionally added a line about what dairy options you could include, if that works for you.

Of course, these days you can find dairy-free alternatives for most milk products, so feel free to add those to suit your taste. Most of the recipes in this book are quite traditional and don't call for any dairy alternatives – even in the baking section. However, there are a handful where I have used dairy-free spread or milk in the method – mostly almond milk as it is a drink that is consumed in Cyprus, Greece and the eastern Mediterranean anyway (we call it *soumada*).

BLESSING THE HOUSE

Blessing the house is common practice amongst many faiths and cultures, and may be familiar to even those who are not religious – I have non-religious friends who cleanse their homes by burning sage bundles. Greek Cypriots will be familiar with a *kapnistiri*, a terracotta chalice like that on the front cover of this book (also opposite, and on page 10). It is made for holding dry, blessed olive leaves and burning them with charcoal; alternatively incense is sometimes used in place of blessed olive leaves. The scented smoke is then used to help bless the house and whoever therein wishes to be blessed. As the smoke rises to heaven, God is asked to receive it and accept it as the prayer rising up before him. There are numerous references to olive leaves in the Bible, and it is not just a symbol in Christianity, it is referred to as a blessed tree in the Qur'an also.

How to fast, or rather, how to use this book

In my day-to-day life I am not always organised when it comes to meals. I often rely on being able to feed myself quickly and deliciously – it's not unhealthy as such, but sometimes nutrition takes a back seat. Of course there are many speedy plant-based meals – a simple tomato pasta takes minutes – but when I am fasting, or want to increase my vegetable intake, life is easier when I do a bit of preparation and have an army of dishes at my disposal during the week. Many of the countries I have drawn recipes from eat in a 'meze' style, with various small plates of food. And I think that is the key when eating a plant-based diet – instead of replicating a 'meat and two veg' meal, it's easier, and I think more appetising, to draw from a few things, made well, and create a harmonious plate of food.

On a Sunday, I often make a selection of cooked and raw dishes and keep them in the fridge or larder so that a nourishing meal is just a few minutes away, with minimal effort. Most of the cooked dishes take no time to prepare, and if the oven is on, you can do a few at once and take the pressure off cooking the following days. Lots of the recipes in this book work well as a mini meze plate, as a filling in a flatbread, or served with a fresh item like fritters or even seafood (if you are eating it).

Here are some of my favourite menu-planning recipes, but many of the dishes will work in this way:

- A bread or recipe from the breakfast chapter – I adore the za'atar buns (page 30), but may just buy some of my favourite pita bread
- Fava (page 178)
- Black-eyed beans (page 181)
- Moutzentra (page 197)
- Prebranac (page 182)
- Braised fennel (page 119)
- Bećar paprikaš (page 116)
- Briam (page 129)
- Cooked root vegetable slaw (page 77)
- Houmous (page 90)
- Muhammara (page 87)
- Dukkah (page 108)

As well as cooked dishes, I make sure I have loads of fresh vegetables and herbs to add fresh flavours:

- Salad leaves
- Tomatoes (please store them out of the fridge)
- Cucumbers (I prefer the little Greek or Middle Eastern ones, but use whatever you can get hold of)
- Mint, coriander, parsley, dill
- Carrots (for coarsely grating and adding to filled pita or salad bowls)

1 — *Breaking bread, breaking fast*

The first meal of the day can vary greatly for Orthodox people who are fasting. Some people like to have a mini meze, with a series of little plates and dishes. For others it may simply be a chunk of bread, slices of ripe tomatoes and some wrinkly black olives with a strong black coffee on the side. Often it is nothing at all. Many of the recipes here are traditional breakfast recipes, and some are inspired by things I like to eat for breakfast, but there is no reason why they can't be eaten at any time. Pulse-based dishes are particularly rewarding in the morning, as they are rich in protein, perfect for keeping you full for longer. But there is nothing to stop you from eating them for dinner.

Lagana: *Clean Monday sesame bread*

This is one of the most symbolic recipes in Greek Orthodox culture. It is a thin crunchy bread that is meant to only be baked on *Kathara Deftera* (Clean Monday), the first day of Easter Lent. Traditionally the bread was unleavened, without yeast, due to the ancient Jews' hasty exodus from Egypt; there wasn't enough time to let the dough rise so it was baked quickly. It is now, however, mostly found made with yeasted dough, not dissimilar to a focaccia. It's very typical to have lagana with taramasalata and olives to start the first big fast of the Orthodox calendar. As *Kathara Deftera* is a major feast day, when families gather, you'll find lagana is often served alongside fasoles (page 186), or some form of beans, including black-eyed beans (page 181), and dolmades, too (page 204).

SERVES 6–8

1 × 7g sachet of fast-action dried yeast
1 tablespoon caster sugar
500g strong white bread flour, plus extra for dusting
¾ teaspoon fine sea salt, plus extra for sprinkling
2 tablespoons olive oil, plus extra for greasing
3 tablespoons sesame seeds

Place the yeast in a measuring jug with half of the caster sugar and top up with 275ml of warm water. Leave to one side for 5 minutes. Place the bread flour in a large mixing bowl, whisk in the sea salt and make a well in the centre. Pour in the yeast water and olive oil and mix into the flour with a fork until it all comes together – add more water if needed; you want a moist dough, not too dry, as it will dry out a little during kneading and proving. Turn the dough out onto a lightly floured surface and knead for 10 minutes, until it is smooth and elastic. If you have a free-standing mixer with a dough hook, do it in that by all means. Transfer the dough to a clean, oiled bowl, cover with a tea towel and leave somewhere warm for 1–1½ hours, to double in size.

When the dough is ready, turn it out onto a lightly floured surface and knock out the air. Lightly oil a large baking or roasting tray, about 30 × 25cm, and stretch the dough in to fit the tin (you can roll with a rolling pin or use your hands). Cover and leave to one side for a second prove to double in size, around 20 minutes.

Meanwhile preheat your oven to 220°C/fan 200°C/gas mark 7. Boil a kettle. When the dough has doubled in size, dissolve the remaining caster sugar in two tablespoons of boiling water. Gently press the dough all over with your fingertips to make little indents all over the surface, then brush with the sugar water. Sprinkle over the sesame seeds and a good pinch of sea salt. Place the tray in the oven and bake for about 20–22 minutes, until golden and crunchy on the outside, and cooked through. Serve in thin slices alongside other Clean Monday favourites.

Little za'atar buns

These swirled buns are my twist on a *manoushe* (*manaqish* when plural), a traditional Levantine morning flatbread that is topped with olive oil and za'atar. They are one of my favourite breakfasts. If I am fasting I will eat them straight up or with a plate of crunchy radishes, cucumbers and olives on the side. When I am not fasting, I might add some labneh, to dip the buns in. You can use a shop-bought za'atar mix, but it is very easy to make your own.

MAKES 9

1 tablespoon caster sugar
1 × 7g sachet of fast-action dried yeast
500g strong white bread flour, plus extra for dusting
¾ teaspoon fine sea salt
125ml extra virgin olive oil, plus extra for greasing
6 tablespoons za'atar (see page 111)
½ teaspoon pul biber

Add the sugar and yeast to a jug and whisk in 275ml of warm water then leave to one side for a couple of minutes. Place the flour in a large mixing bowl and whisk in the salt, then make a well in the centre. Mix in the yeast water and 25ml of the extra virgin olive oil until well combined – add more water if needed; you want a moist dough, it shouldn't be too dry. Transfer the dough to a flour-dusted surface and knead for around 8–10 minutes, until smooth and elastic. Wash and dry the mixing bowl, then lightly oil it. Return it to the bowl, drizzle with a little more oil and leave to prove for around 1–1½ hours (this will depend on how warm your kitchen is), until doubled in size.

When the dough has risen, turn it out onto a clean surface, knock it back and roll into a rectangle about 26 × 40cm. Brush over a layer of olive oil and evenly sprinkle over the za'atar and pul biber, leaving a 1cm border around the edges. Pat the spice mixture gently into the dough with the back of a tablespoon. Starting with a short side, roll the dough up as tightly as you can. Trim off the uneven excess bits at the end. Slice the dough into 9 pieces. Pour enough oil to just cover the base of a 23cm square cake tin and pop in the slices, swirl facing up. Cover and leave to one side for a second prove to double in size, about 30 minutes.

Meanwhile, preheat the oven to 200°C/fan 180°C/gas mark 6. When the buns have roughly doubled in size, bake for 25–30 minutes, until golden. As soon as they come out of the oven, drizzle over the remaining olive oil and leave to absorb in the tin for 10 minutes before serving.

Covrigi: *salty poppy seed twists*

While these Romanian twisted breads may look intimidating I can assure you that once you have mastered basic bread dough they really are quite simple (and satisfying to make). You can have fun with the shapes – the twisted ones are my favourite. And while the addition of onion flakes and sesame seeds may not be traditional, I do enjoy the bagel vibes they give, especially as the dough is briefly boiled in the same way that bagels and pretzels are. Romanian food writer Irina Georgescu told me that pretzel-style covrigi has a modern influence from Middle Eastern and Jewish bakers. Traditionally the twisted dough is left to prove and then baked like bread. You can of course follow this process, however there is something about the shape of covrigi that just lends itself so well to the chewiness that boiling the dough brings.

MAKES 8

- 1 tablespoon caster sugar
- 1 × 7g sachet of fast-action dried yeast
- 500g strong white bread flour, plus extra for dusting
- 1 teaspoon fine sea salt
- 3 tablespoons olive or sunflower oil
- 2 tablespoons bicarbonate of soda
- 1 tablespoon poppy seeds
- 1 tablespoon sesame seeds
- ¾ teaspoon flaky sea salt
- 1 tablespoon onion flakes

Place the caster sugar in a measuring jug with the yeast and stir in 260ml of warm water. Whisk and leave to one side for 5 minutes. Place the flour in a large mixing bowl and whisk in the fine sea salt. Make a well in the centre, and whisk the yeast water into the flour with a fork. Add two tablespoons of the oil and bring the dough together. Turn it out onto a lightly floured surface and knead for 5–10 minutes, until the dough is smooth and elastic. Transfer to a lightly greased clean bowl and leave to prove for 1–1½ hours, or until doubled in size.

When the dough is ready, turn it out onto your work top and knock out the air. Divide into eight even-sized pieces. For a traditional pretzel shape, roll each piece into a 50cm long sausage. Fold the ends into the centre, crossing them over to create a heart shape, and pinch them in place. For the twirled shape, cut a piece of the dough in half and roll both pieces into a 35cm long sausage. Pinch the ends together and twist the strips, then join the ends together to create a ring. Transfer to two lightly oiled baking sheets and leave to prove until doubled in size, about 20 minutes.

Preheat your oven to 220°C/fan 200°C/gas mark 7. Bring a large pan of water to the boil and add the bicarbonate of soda to the water. In a bowl, mix together the poppy seeds, sesame seeds, flaky sea salt and onion flakes. Using a large mesh strainer, submerge the pretzels into the water for 30 seconds, then let the moisture dry off them and return them to their trays. When they are all done, brush with the remaining olive or sunflower oil and sprinkle liberally with the spice mix – patting it in place. Bake in the oven for around 18–20 minutes, until deeply golden brown but still fluffy in the middle. Leave to one side to cool (if you can wait).

Koulouri: *Cypriot village bread*

In my dough world, koulouri is queen, the best of breads – nothing beats a just-out-the-oven, warm koulouri. I'm aware there are a few hard-to-find ingredients used here, and although you can make it without them, for a truly authentic Cypriot koulouri experience you do need them. Aniseed is key – just a few seeds on the outside will add that subtle, but important, flavour.

MAKES 1 LOAF

1 × 7g sachet of fast-action dried yeast
1½ tablespoons caster sugar
1 piece of mastic
2 pieces of mehlepi
500g strong white bread flour, plus extra for dusting
1 teaspoon fine sea salt
¼ teaspoon ground cinnamon
2 tablespoons olive oil, plus extra for greasing
4 tablespoons sesame seeds
2 teaspoons nigella seeds
½ teaspoon aniseed

Pour 330ml of warm water into a measuring jug and whisk in the yeast and a tablespoon of the caster sugar. Leave to one side for a couple of minutes. Meanwhile, grind the mastic and then mehlepi separately, each with a teaspoon of flour until finely ground. Place the rest of the flour (minus one tablespoon) with the sea salt, ground cinnamon, ground mastic and ground mehlepi into a large mixing bowl and whisk together. Make a well in the centre, pour in the yeast water, along with the olive oil, and whisk it with a fork. You may need to add a further two or three tablespoons of water at this point if your dough isn't coming together. It's better to have a slightly wetter dough, rather than too dry. When it has all come together, turn the dough out onto a lightly floured surface and knead it for 10 minutes. Try not to over-flour the surface or dough, as it will become more elastic as you work it. Transfer the kneaded dough to a clean, lightly oiled bowl, cover with a clean tea towel and leave in a warm place to prove. It will take 1–1½ hours to double in size.

When the dough is ready, turn it out onto a clean surface and knock it back. Roll it into a long sausage, around 30cm, and place it diagonally on an oiled baking sheet. Using a sharp knife or dough cutter, cut the dough into 10 pieces, and very gently pull them apart so there is a 2mm gap between each piece. Whisk the reserved tablespoon of flour with two tablespoons of warm water to create a loose paste and brush the dough all over. Mix the sesame seeds in a bowl with the nigella seeds and aniseed and pat all over the dough – it may look like a lot, but you want a really even crust, with some underneath too if you can. Cover with a tea towel and prove again until doubled in size, about 30 minutes.

Preheat your oven to 220°C/fan 200°C/gas mark 7. Boil a kettle. Pour 150ml of boiling water in a small ovenproof dish. When you place the bread in the oven, place the dish at the bottom also. Leave in the oven for at least 22–25 minutes before checking. It should be golden brown all over. Leave to cool for at least 10 minutes, before tucking in.

Fatayer muhammara: *smoky red pepper and walnut flatbreads*

Muhammara is a delicious dip, and here it acts as a wonderful topping for flatbreads. The end result is warm delicious flatbreads that don't look and feel a million miles away from *lahmacun* (thin Turkish breads topped with tomato and minced meat). So although you need to make the full muhammara recipe to make these fatayer, it's not that hard and the leftovers will keep in your fridge for a few days.

MAKES 8

- 1 tablespoon caster sugar
- 1 × 7g sachet of fast-action dried yeast
- 350g strong white bread flour, plus extra for dusting
- ½ teaspoon fine sea salt
- 4 tablespoons olive oil, plus extra for greasing
- ½ × batch of muhammara (see page 87)
- 1 pomegranate
- ½ bunch of flat-leaf parsley
- A few mint sprigs
- 4 tablespoons pomegranate molasses

Place the caster sugar and yeast in a jug then stir in 200ml of warm water and leave to one side for a few minutes. Lightly oil a mixing bowl and a couple of baking trays. In another large mixing bowl whisk together the flour and sea salt and make a well in the middle. Pour in the yeast water and two tablespoons of the olive oil and mix it in with a fork so it comes together, adding a little more water if it feels too dry. Turn the dough out onto a lightly floured surface and knead for 10 minutes, until smooth and elastic. Transfer it to a clean, lightly oiled bowl, and leave to prove for 1–1½ hours, or until the dough has doubled in size.

Meanwhile, make the muhammara as instructed on page 87. When the dough is ready, knock out the air and roll into a sausage. Cut the dough into 8 pieces and roll each piece out into a circle, around 12cm. Lay the circles out on the lightly greased baking trays and top each with a heaped tablespoon of muhammara. Spread the muhammara out into a thin layer, leaving a 1cm border around the edge. Leave to prove again for 20 minutes.

Meanwhile, preheat your oven to 220°C/fan 200°C/gas mark 7. Drizzle each flatbread with a little oil. Bake in the oven for 18–20 minutes, or until golden and cooked through. While they are baking, carefully pick the pomegranate seeds. Pick and roughly chop the parsley and mint leaves. When the flatbreads are ready, drizzle with the pomegranate molasses, sprinkle over the pomegranate seeds and chopped herbs and serve warm.

Bobalki: *Christmas dough balls, two ways*

These Slovak Christmas dough balls are traditionally eaten on Christmas Eve as part of a twelve-course meatless meal, where each course represents one of the apostles. It is such an intriguing recipe: the balls are baked until golden and crisp, then are doused in boiling water, before being tumbled in a sweet or savoury topping. The key is to coat them in only just enough water to soften them but not so much that they become soggy.

Here I've given two options to flavour the bobalki: tangy sauerkraut and onion, or sticky honey and poppy seeds. Honey is often used in traditional Orthodox fasting recipes, but in this book I have tried to be considerate to those following a vegan lifestyle and give alternatives. This is one of a few recipes where I don't. I've made them with substitutions, but I just don't think they work as well or taste as good. If you must, a simple sugar syrup, with the addition of the juice from half a lemon, will work OK.

MAKES 60–70

- 1 × 7g sachet of fast-action dried yeast
- 1 tablespoon caster sugar
- 500g strong white bread flour, plus extra for dusting
- ¾ teaspoon fine sea salt
- 3 tablespoons olive oil, plus extra for greasing

Sauerkraut, onion and caraway

- 3 onions
- 3 tbsp olive oil
- 1 heaped teaspoon caraway seeds
- 150g sauerkraut
- Sea salt and freshly ground black pepper

Honey, lemon and poppy seed

- 3 tablespoons poppy seeds
- 1 lemon
- 150ml honey (see introduction)

Place the yeast in a measuring jug with the caster sugar and whisk in 275ml of warm water. Leave to one side for 5 minutes. Place the flour in a large mixing bowl, whisk in the sea salt and make a well in the centre. Pour in the yeast water and olive oil and mix in with a fork until it all comes together. Turn the dough out onto a lightly floured surface and knead for 10 minutes, until it is smooth and elastic. If you have a free-standing mixer with a dough hook, you can use that if you prefer. Transfer the dough to a clean, lightly oiled bowl, cover with a tea towel and leave somewhere warm for 1–1½ hours, until double in size.

Lightly oil a large roasting tray; if you don't have a very large one, oil a couple. When the dough is ready, turn it out onto a lightly floured surface and knock out the air. Roll the dough out to a 2.5cm-thick sausage and cut into small, even pieces, so that when you roll them they're balls about 2.5cm. Place them all on a lightly oiled baking tray, so they are all just touching. Cover and leave to one side for a second prove to double in size, about 30 minutes.

Meanwhile, preheat your oven to 220°C/fan 200°C/gas mark 7. When the dough balls have roughly doubled in size, bake for 18–20 minutes, or until golden and cooked through. Remove from the oven and leave to cool before combining with one of the two toppings.

For the sauerkraut, onion and caraway bobalki: Peel and finely chop the onions. Place a medium frying pan on medium-low and pour in the olive oil. Add the chopped onions and caraway seeds and season generously with salt and pepper. Sauté for 12–15 minutes, until soft and lightly browned. Drain and chop the sauerkraut and add to the pan. Turn the heat up a little and fry for a further 3 minutes, until golden.

When ready, break the dough balls apart and place in a large colander directly in the sink. Boil your kettle and pour enough just-boiled water over the balls to soften them slightly, but not turn them mushy (you can do this in batches if easier). Drain the balls and place in a large mixing bowl or tray and spoon over the sauerkraut mixture. Toss together well.

For the honey, lemon and poppy seed bobalki: Place the poppy seeds in a mortar and finely grate in the lemon zest. Grind just enough with a pestle so they release their flavours but retain a good seedy texture, and keep to one side. Pour the honey into a small saucepan and squeeze in the juice of half the lemon. Warm over a medium heat.

When ready, break the dough balls apart and place in a large colander directly in the sink. Boil your kettle and pour enough just-boiled water over the balls to soften them slightly, but not turn them mushy (you can do this in batches). Drain the balls and place in a large mixing bowl or tray and pour over the warm lemony honey. Sprinkle over the ground poppy seeds and toss with your hands to coat the bread completely.

Serve the bobalki straight away, or chill until needed.

(Photos overleaf)

Left to right: honey, lemon and poppy seed bobalki; sauerkraut, onion and caraway bobalki (pages 38–39)

Eliopites: *olive, mint and coriander buns*

Eliopites, or *eliotes*, are little herby olive buns that are a staple in Greek and Cypriot kitchens. Some cooks prefer to keep the stones in the olives, as it retains more flavour. That may be true, but it's a game of Russian roulette my teeth and I are not willing to play, so I use pitted olives. In terms of bread baking, they require very little effort, with maximum return on flavour.

MAKES 12

175g pitted black olives
2 onions
4 mint sprigs
½ bunch of coriander
1 tablespoon caster sugar
1 × 7g sachet of fast-action dried yeast
500g strong white bread flour, plus extra for dusting
¾ teaspoon fine sea salt
100ml olive oil, plus extra for greasing

Tear the olives in half. Peel and finely chop the onions. Pick and finely slice the mint leaves. Finely slice the coriander leaves and stalks. Mix everything together and leave to one side. Mix the sugar and yeast in a jug with 225ml of warm water. In a large bowl whisk together the flour and salt and pour in the olive oil, rubbing it in with your fingers to create breadcrumbs. Slowly pour in the yeast water, mixing it in until you have a wet dough, adding more water if it feels a little dry. Knead it for a few minutes then add the herby olive and onion mixture and mix in. Turn it out onto a flour-dusted surface, and knead for 10 minutes until smooth. Return the dough to a clean, oiled bowl, cover with a tea towel and leave in a warm spot for around 1–1½ hours, or until doubled in size.

Once the dough is ready, turn it out onto a clean surface and knock out the air. Knead it for a further minute or two then divide the dough into 12 pieces and shape them into rolls. Place on an oiled baking tray, cover with a tea towel and leave to prove again for a further 30 minutes, or until doubled in size.

Meanwhile, preheat your oven to full whack. When the buns have doubled in size, bake for 20–25 minutes, turning the temperature down to 220°C/fan 200°C/gas mark 7 as soon as they go in. They are ready when they are golden brown, and cooked through. Leave to cool for at least 10 minutes before serving.

The Mount Athos monks and why they eat at 9am...

I have been fortunate enough to chat to a few priests and monks while researching my book – Father Theona in Mount Athos, my uncle Father Andreas in Cyprus, Father Augustine in Lebanon and Father John here in London. And although it may come as no surprise that most of them do not eat breakfast while fasting, it transpires that the monks on Mount Athos do in fact eat in the morning. This was a shock to me, as I imagined them to be the most strict. However it is due to the fact that Mount Athos priests do not adhere to the same times as we do. Their days are based on the solar day, known as Byzantine time. Their day begins at sunset, when the clock is zeroed, rather than at midnight. And with the changes in length of day and daylight throughout the seasons, the hour zero can vary greatly during the year. So while the monks do eat at around 9am, this meal is technically their lunch, with their mid-afternoon meal mirroring what we call 'dinner'. To the monks these meals are simply referred to as the 'morning meal' and 'evening meal'.

Koliva (page 46)

Koliva: *sweet memorial offering*

If you have ever attended a Greek Orthodox church service, you may be familiar with koliva. There are always trays of it at the front of the church, waiting to be blessed by the priest, then spooned into bags and handed to parishioners as they leave. It is made as part of a loved one's memorial (*mnemosyno*) or funeral, as well as during times of fasting like Great Lent and Christmas. However, you may also recognise it as *kollyva* or *colivă* – as it is a feature in many countries of Orthodox faith, including Bulgaria, Romania and Serbia.

Each country has their variations, but the constant seems to be the boiled wheat grains at the centre of the dish. These are then tossed with any combinations of sesame seeds, raisins, aniseed, almonds, walnuts, cinnamon, pomegranate seeds, honey, rum, icing sugar, cocoa, silver dragée decorations and other sweets. The mixture is served in a mound on an oval platter, to resemble a grave, and then traditionally covered in icing sugar. This is then decorated with more nuts, pomegranate seeds or silver balls, and will often spell out the initials of the person being remembered.

In some Orthodox countries (but not Greece and Cyprus), you will even find a dish like this in pudding-form. It is sometimes called *berbara*, for the St Barbara's feast day in December, and anoush abour (page 254) at New Year.

While koliva may look simple, it is actually quite technical and needs to be made properly, due to the risk of the wheat fermenting (which can be dangerous to anyone who ingests it). As a result you'll find churches and villages sometimes have a designated maker, who you commission to make it for you. Don't let this put you off though, just be sure that your grains are thoroughly dry before placing them in the fridge.

(Photo on previous page)

SERVES MANY

350g whole wheat grains
200g skin-on almonds (you can buy them blanched but this method means you end up splitting them in half too)
100g sesame seeds
250g sultanas
2 pomegranates
2 teaspoons aniseed
1 tablespoon ground cinnamon
Icing sugar, optional
Silver dragée decorations, optional

On the Friday night before you want to take this to be blessed, soak the whole wheat grains and almonds in separate bowls in plenty of cold water. Leave until the next day. Then when you are ready, place the wheat grains in a pan of fresh water over a high heat and bring to the boil, then reduce the heat and simmer for 30 minutes, or until the grains have cooked and start to split in half. Drain in a colander and then leave them to cool and dry. Line a tray with kitchen paper and spread the cooked wheat out so the paper fully absorbs any moisture. When the wheat is dry, transfer to a bowl, then discard damp kitchen paper and replace with new. Spread the wheat evenly out on the freshly lined tray, then place the tray, uncovered, in the fridge.

For the almonds, keep them in their bowl of water while you peel off or pop them out of their skins. This is quite time consuming but also therapeutic. Encourage them to split in half, also. Then, place the peeled halved almonds in a fresh bowl of cold water and in the fridge also. Place the sesame seeds in a small sieve and wash under cold running water. Place the sieve over a bowl and leave in the fridge to drain and dry. Wash the sultanas in a colander then leave to drain and dry in the sink. Spread them out on a kitchen paper-lined tray or plate and store in the fridge. (Greeks wash everything. I imagine this is to do with how things were stored in the old times. I don't know if there is such a good reason to do it now, but I do it anyway.) Carefully remove the seeds from the pomegranates, discarding the pith and skin, and keep in a covered container in the fridge.

On the Sunday morning of the memorial, put together your koliva. You may want to keep some of the almonds, sesame seeds, pomegranate seeds and sultanas aside for decoration. Place the rest of them in a large bowl with the cooked wheat, aniseed and cinnamon and mix together well. Spoon onto an oval tray that has a lip all around the edge, and pat out evenly. You can then decorate how you wish – it is common to either spell out the initials of the person you are remembering, or mark a cross. You can adorn the koliva directly or coat it in icing sugar first; it is up to you.

Tahini, cinnamon and carob pancakes

Carob is a historic staple of Cypriot agriculture, and my paternal yiayia is from Limassol, an area famous for its carob trees, with an ancient carob mill at the centre of the old town. I grew up with bottles of the syrup – 'black gold' – in the family kitchens, ready to be used in baking and drinks. Tahini, cinnamon and carob is a dream flavour combination in my eyes; sweetened tahini drizzled with a touch of carob is the perfect adornment for pancakes. And with this topping being naturally *nistisimo*, making the pancakes egg-free means this is a treat breakfast to enjoy even while fasting.

Carob syrup is rich, and a little goes a long way. If you haven't tried carob, it is often compared to chocolate. It's a subtle similarity; they are both dark and intense, so I get the comparison but I enjoy carob in its own right.

SERVES 4

250g plain flour
2 tablespoons caster sugar
½ teaspoon ground cinnamon
¼ teaspoon fine sea salt
500ml milk of your choice (oat and almond work well)
2 tablespoons olive or vegetable oil, plus extra for greasing
5 tablespoons tahini
3 tablespoons honey (or caster sugar)
2 tablespoons carob syrup
2 bananas, optional

Place the plain flour in a large mixing bowl and whisk in the caster sugar, the cinnamon and half the sea salt. Make a well in the middle and whisk in the milk and oil until smooth. It should be the consistency of double cream – if it is a little thick add a splash more milk. Leave the batter to rest in the fridge for half an hour if possible. Put a kettle on. In a small bowl, mix the tahini with three or four tablespoons of just-boiled water until smooth, then stir in the honey and the rest of the salt. Set aside.

When you are ready to make your pancakes, place a large non-stick frying pan on a medium heat. Drizzle in a touch of oil, and use kitchen paper to spread it over the pan. You don't want too much oil, just enough to cover the base. When the pan is hot, ladle in the batter and tilt the pan so it covers the base. The first pancake often goes a bit wrong – chef's perks for snacking – but it will help you figure out how much batter you need to cover your pan. Cook for a few minutes until lightly golden underneath, then flip over. Because there is no egg in the mixture, they don't quite brown the way regular pancakes do, but you will know when they are ready. Cook for a further minute or two, then serve or transfer to a plate. You can either serve the pancakes as you go, drizzling them with the sweetened tahini and then the carob syrup on top, or cook all the batter and keep them warm on a plate in a low oven. Repeat with all the batter, rubbing a little oil on the base of the pan every so often. If you've kept the pancakes warm as you've cooked them, arrange them on a platter and, when ready, drizzle the tahini and carob over the lot. I like them with sliced banana – I think it works well with the nutty sweet tahini and rich carob, but that is up to you.

Ful medames: *creamy, spiced fava beans*

You can keep your beans on toast, ful medames and balila (page 52) are exactly the kind of nutritious and flavoursome meals I want to start my day with. Ful medames started as a traditional breakfast in Egypt and is popular throughout the Middle East. Cooking the beans the day before (or using tinned) makes this a quick breakfast option. You could even make the whole thing the day before and just warm through when you want to eat it.

SERVES 2 FOR BREAKFAST, 4 AS PART OF A MEZE

250g dried split fava beans, or 2 × 400g tins of cooked beans (if fava beans are hard to come by, you can use cannellini, haricot or borlotti beans)
1 onion
3 garlic cloves
Extra virgin olive oil
½ teaspoon ground cumin
Sea salt and freshly ground black pepper
1 large green chilli
½ bunch of flat-leaf parsley
1–2 lemons
2 ripe tomatoes

To serve: Pita bread, cucumber, spring onions and black olives

If you are making this from scratch, wash the dried fava beans, discard any stones, and leave to soak overnight in plenty of cold water. Then when you are ready to cook them, place in a pan with 5 times as much fresh cold water and bring to a boil. Reduce the heat, and simmer gently for 2 hours, or until tender and cooked through. Check them occasionally to make sure they haven't boiled dry. Drain the cooked beans but reserve a large mug of the cooking water.

If you're using tinned beans, start here: drain them and reserve the liquid.

Peel and finely chop the onion and garlic. Place a large frying pan on a medium-low heat. Add two tablespoons of olive oil, the chopped onion and half the chopped garlic; sauté for 10 minutes till the onions are soft but not coloured. Stir in the cumin then add the drained fava plus about 200ml of the cooking/tin water. Bring to the boil, season, then reduce the heat to low for around 10 minutes. Towards the end of cooking, especially if you're using tinned beans, you might need to use a potato masher to gently mash the beans. You don't want a purée, just a creamy broken consistency – you can add a little more liquid here if need be.

While the beans are cooking, make the dressing. Halve and finely chop the chilli (for a milder dressing you can remove the seeds) and place in a mortar with the remaining garlic and a good pinch of salt. Bash with the pestle until broken down, smoother and well combined. Roughly chop the parsley, then add that to the mortar and pound it in. Halve one lemon and squeeze in its juice, then stir in a couple of tablespoons of oil to loosen to your taste. Halve and deseed the tomatoes, and finely chop the flesh.

Serve the creamy fava beans drizzled with the spicy green dressing over the top and scattered with the chopped tomatoes. Cut the remaining lemon into wedges and serve on the side. Perfect with warm pita bread, sticks of cucumber, chopped spring onions and olives.

Balila: *crushed garlicky chickpeas with asparagus*

It's a faff, but balila is particularly good when the chickpeas are peeled; it makes them creamier and smoother. To make a more authentic balila, leave out the asparagus. However, I love asparagus – both the wild asparagus we get in Cyprus and the cultivated English kind – and enjoy cooking it as simply as possible. Having it folded through balila, the way you might add it to scrambled eggs, felt like a natural combination.

SERVES 2 FOR BREAKFAST, 4 AS PART OF A MEZE

500g cooked chickpeas (see page 289), or 2 × 400g jars/tins of chickpeas
4 garlic cloves
250g asparagus
4 tablespoons extra virgin olive oil, plus extra for drizzling
1 teaspoon ground cumin
½ lemon
Sea salt and freshly ground black pepper
½ bunch of flat-leaf parsley

If cooking your own chickpeas, get those ready and keep to one side, along with the cooking liquid.

Peel and finely chop the garlic. Snap the woody ends off the asparagus stalks and discard them. Finely slice the stalks – I like to keep the tips whole and sliced in half lengthways. Place the olive oil in a medium saucepan over a medium-low heat and add the garlic and asparagus. Fry the vegetables for 5 minutes, then add the ground cumin. Fry for 2 minutes, then add chickpeas and 200ml of the cooking water. If you are using tinned chickpeas, just add the liquid from the tins. Increase the heat to high and bring to the boil, and use the back of a fork to crush about a third of the chickpeas and make the mixture a little creamy. Reduce the heat to medium and simmer for 10 minutes. Squeeze in the juice from the lemon half, season generously and continue to cook for 5 more minutes. Meanwhile, finely chop the parsley. When the chickpeas look creamy and thick, the balila is ready. Taste and adjust the seasoning as needed, then spoon into a serving dish. Finish by drizzling with extra virgin olive oil and scattering over the chopped parsley. This can be served warm or at room temperature.

Pisiseeh: *sautéed bread in garlic oil*

This unusual recipe was taught to me by Suat Inan, who lives in the Netherlands but whose family is from Arnas, a tiny village in Tür Abdin in the south-east of Turkey, close to the Syrian border. Her Syriac Orthodox family fasted not only before the big religious holidays but every Wednesday and Friday, and this recipe featured regularly. Her family were farmers and lived off the land, and she describes the winters as 'freezing cold, and the summers hot as hell' which meant plenty of making do and eating whatever the land and seasons provided. I imagine in those brutal winters this would be exactly the kind of comforting dish you'd need – not to mention thrifty, tasty and easy to make if you were cooking for a family with ten children, as Suat's mother did.

As a recipe writer, being taught a recipe that you can't find any research on is rare, and I have not been able to find anything on pisiseeh. Suat and her mother don't know this by any other name, and have never seen this recipe written anywhere they so have spelled the name how it is said. To be able to include pisiseeh here, and pass it on to future generations on behalf of Suat's family, is an honour.

Although the dukkah and chilli aren't included in Suat's original recipe, I enjoy the warmth they bring to the dish.

SERVES 2

- 4 garlic cloves
- 2 stale large pita breads, or ½ stale Turkish pide
- 4 tablespoons olive oil
- Sea salt and freshly ground black pepper
- 1 tablespoon dukkah (see page 108), optional
- A few pinches of pul biber or dried chilli flakes, optional

Peel and finely chop the garlic. Tear the stale pita or pide into small, bite-sized pieces. Boil a kettle of water so you have hot water ready to go. Place the olive oil in a medium saucepan over a low heat and add the chopped garlic. Fry for a minute or two; it shouldn't go crispy, you want it just cooked enough to infuse the oil and start to turn golden, then stir in the torn bread. Turn the heat up a little and fry the bread for a minute, stirring to coat in the garlicky oil. Slowly add 250ml of the boiled water, stir until absorbed, and add a further 100–200ml of water, so the bread is soft but not too soupy. Season generously with salt and black pepper, and finish with the dukkah and a pinch of pul biber or dried chilli flakes, if you like.

Makdous: *baby aubergines with walnuts and chilli*

Baby aubergines, stuffed with pepper, chilli, garlic and walnuts and then cured in olive oil, are a popular fasting (or any time) breakfast throughout the eastern Mediterranean and Middle East. However, like so many of the recipes in this chapter, makdous is good at any time of the day. Traditionally, preserving the aubergines takes at least a day; my cooked version is heartier but relatively simple to put together – making a more immediate, still delicious, meal.

SERVES 2–4

5 garlic cloves
1 red chilli
1 red pepper
Olive oil
1 × 400g tin of chopped tomatoes
Sea salt and freshly ground black pepper
1 tablespoon red wine vinegar
125g walnuts
½ bunch of coriander
½ teaspoon dried chilli flakes
½ teaspoon ground cinnamon
½ teaspoon ground cumin
½ teaspoon ground coriander
10 baby aubergines

Peel the garlic cloves, and finely slice two of them. Halve the chilli, remove the seeds and finely slice. Halve the pepper, remove the seeds and chop into 1cm pieces. Pour two tablespoons of olive oil into a medium saucepan and place over a medium-low heat. Add the sliced garlic and fry for a couple of minutes, then add half the sliced chilli and all the chopped pepper. Sauté for 10 minutes, then stir in the tin of chopped tomatoes and season well. Fill the tin with water, add to the pan and bring to the boil. When it starts to bubble, reduce the heat and stir in the vinegar. Simmer for 15 minutes, until the sauce has thickened a little.

While the sauce is simmering, make the aubergine stuffing. Place the three remaining garlic cloves into a food processor along with the walnuts. Cut off the coriander stalks and add them to the food processor, reserving the leaves. Add the dried chilli flakes, ground cinnamon, ground cumin and ground coriander and season well. Blitz everything together until finely chopped then add just enough olive oil to bring the mixture together. Leaving the stalks intact, slice the aubergines in half lengthways twice, so that it is in quarters, but is still connected by the stalk. Stuff the inside of the aubergines with the walnut mixture, a couple of teaspoons in each. This is easiest done with your hands to compress the nuts inside. Reserve any remaining mixture for the sauce.

Place a large frying pan on a medium-low heat and add four tablespoons of olive oil. Gently lay in the aubergines and fry for 8–10 minutes, until softened on one side, then turn them over and fry on the other side for 5 minutes. At this stage you can either carefully remove the aubergines to a plate, spoon the pepper-tomato sauce into the frying pan and place the aubergines on the sauce. Or you can spoon the sauce around the aubergines, nestling them in. Dot in any remaining walnut mixture, cover the pan with a lid and simmer for 15 minutes, by which point the aubergines should be tender. Roughly chop the reserved coriander leaves and scatter over the top before serving.

Fattet houmous

If you love houmous, you must try this. Fattet (or fatteh) houmous is popular throughout the Middle East, where you will find variations not only on spelling but toppings. It usually has a yoghurt-tahini sauce component, but when fasting I replace that with a simple tahini-lemon dressing, a bit like the tashi you will find on page 94. You can add a dairy-free yoghurt if that is your bag, and I won't judge you if you use a good-quality shop-bought houmous here – that way this becomes a breakfast you can put together in the time it takes to brew a coffee.

SERVES 6

1 × quantity of houmous (see page 90), or about 600g good-quality shop-bought houmous
4 pita breads
Olive oil
Sea salt and freshly ground black pepper
50g pine nuts
70g tahini
1 lemon
2 garlic cloves
½ bunch of flat-leaf parsley
1 green chilli
100g radishes
½ pomegranate
2 tablespoons pomegranate molasses
½ teaspoon sumac

To serve: Fresh bread

Make the houmous as instructed on page 90, and if you're cooking the chickpeas from scratch, reserve 125ml of the cooking water.

Preheat your oven to 180°C/fan 160°C/gas mark 4. Cut the pita bread into 2.5cm squares and lay out on a baking tray. Drizzle the bread with a little olive oil and season with salt and pepper. Scatter the pine nuts into a small baking dish and place it and the baking tray in the oven. Remove the pine nuts after 7 minutes, when golden, and bake the pita squares for a further 8 minutes, until they are golden also.

Meanwhile, spoon the tahini into a large mixing bowl and juice the lemon. Boil a kettle. Stir the lemon juice and 100ml boiling water into the tahini (add an additional few tablespoons if it is quite thick; it should have the consistency of double cream). Peel the garlic cloves then finely grate them straight into the bowl, and season generously. Whisk together and taste, adjusting the seasoning as needed. Finely chop the parsley leaves and stalks. Halve, deseed and finely slice the chilli. Trim and finely slice the radishes. Pick the pomegranate seeds and keep to one side.

To assemble the fattet houmous, toss the toasted pita with the reserved 125ml of chickpea water (alternatively, you can use boiling water) and spread two-thirds of it into a large serving dish. Spoon over the houmous, then scatter over the remaining pita squares and half of the radishes. Drizzle over the tahini dressing. Scatter over the remaining radishes and drizzle with the pomegranate molasses. Garnish with the chopped parsley, the pomegranate seeds, sumac and sliced chilli. Serve straight away, with fresh bread for mopping up all the dressing.

Galayet bandora: *fried tomatoes*

This simple Jordanian dish is usually served as part of a larger meal. I chose to include it in the breakfast chapter as it is precisely the kind of light but flavoursome food I love to eat in the morning – although you could include as part of a breakfast meze scenario. Add some toasted bread or pita and it hits the same notes as *pan con tomate* in Spain, and, if you are not fasting, a boiled egg or chunk of feta on the side would work, too.

SERVES 4 AS A LIGHT BREAKFAST, OR PART OF A MEZE

1kg ripe tomatoes
2 onions
3 garlic cloves
4 tablespoons olive oil
2 green chillies
Sea salt and freshly ground black pepper

To serve: A few sprigs each of flat-leaf parsley and mint, slices of bread or pita, extra virgin olive oil,

Peel the tomatoes (see page 287) and then roughly each one, discarding the core but keeping the seeds. Peel and finely chop the onions and garlic cloves. Place the olive oil in a wide saucepan or large frying pan over a low heat. Add the chopped onion and garlic and fry for 10 minutes, until soft and translucent. For a gentle chilli heat, pierce the two chillies all over with the tip of your knife and add them to the pan, along with the tomatoes. If you like it fiery, deseed then finely chop one or both chillies before adding them and the tomatoes to the pan. Season well and turn the heat up a little. Fry for 15–20 minutes, stirring often, until the tomatoes have softened and thickened and juice has reduced.

When the tomatoes are almost ready, pick and finely chop the parsley and mint leaves. Toast the bread or pita, if you like, and drizzle with extra virgin olive oil. Sprinkle the herbs over the top of the tomatoes, and serve with the bread on the side.

2 *Salads, dips and pickles*

In the eastern Mediterranean you will almost always find a salad as part of a larger meal. We think nothing about eating a hot dish such as moutzentra (lentils) or a rice dish like spanakorizo with a side of salad, especially one with a punchy, acidic dressing to cut through the hot food. However, we also appreciate a salad in its own right, especially substantial ones that involve grains, lentils or pasta, which makes them perfect for a light meal. And our dips can be a snack, but also act as a vegetable side. I find that when rich or savoury flavours are missing from a lack of dairy or meat, I like to ramp up the flavour of dressings. Herbs, spices and considered extra toppings become crucial. The onion oil (page 106) is a great recipe to have in your arsenal to vamp up the simplest of vegetables. And dukkah (page 108) is a popular way of adding maximum texture and flavour to almost any dish. A jar on your shelf will save the day time and again.

Broad bean, dill and tomato salad

One of my happiest memories is podding broad beans with my yiayia, an experience that seems to resonate for many people. Frozen broad beans are available year-round, but taking the time to prepare them in season has to be one of the simplest kitchen joys, and makes the recipe taste all the sweeter. This simple salad is far greater than the sum of its parts. Be sure to be generous with the seasoning and serve with fresh, crusty bread – koulouri or Lebanese flatbread if you can. It may not look like a vast amount, but the beans are surprisingly filling. If you are not fasting, then a chunk of feta on top is a welcome addition.

SERVES 4

1.5kg broad beans (350–400g podded weight)
4 spring onions
1 lemon
3 tablespoons extra virgin olive oil
Sea salt and freshly ground black pepper
1 bunch of dill
3 ripe tomatoes
½ garlic clove

To serve: Fresh bread, ideally koulouri (page 35)

Pod the broad beans. Bring a pan of water to the boil and blanch the beans for 2½–3 minutes, depending on their size. Drain and immediately transfer to a bowl of ice water. Leave them for 5 minutes, then remove the opaque skins, so that you are just left with the vibrant green beans inside. Trim and finely slice the spring onions and toss through the broad beans, along with the juice of the lemon, and two tablespoons of the extra virgin olive oil and a generous pinch each of sea salt and freshly ground black pepper. Finely chop the dill and stir through. Check the seasoning and leave to one side.

Place a box grater in a large shallow bowl and grate in the flesh and seeds of the tomatoes on the coarsest side; discard the skins. Finely grate in the peeled garlic clove, then stir in the final tablespoon of extra virgin olive oil and season to taste. When the dressing is ready, pile the dressed broad beans on top of the grated tomatoes and serve with fresh bread.

Roast tomato, orzo and rocket salad with roasted garlic dressing

This pasta salad screams summer, from slow-cooking a glut of sweet ripe tomatoes, to the thrown-together nature of the rest of the ingredients – it is exactly what you want in your lunchbox on a picnic. You could of course adorn it with crumbled feta, or even coarsely grated halloumi, however it is robust and flavoursome enough without any dairy. (Also, who likes sweaty cheese on a picnic. No thanks.)

SERVES 4–6

750g ripe tomatoes – a mixture of sizes and types
4 garlic cloves
Olive oil
Sea salt and freshly ground black pepper
½ tablespoon dried oregano
75g pine nuts
250g orzo
2 tablespoons red wine vinegar
1 heaped teaspoon Dijon mustard
3 tablespoons extra virgin olive oil
1 bunch of basil (use Greek basil if you have access to it)
50g wild rocket

Preheat your oven to 170°C/fan 150°C/gas mark 3½. Chop the tomatoes: halve any smaller ones and cut any larger ones into quarters. Lay them out in a roasting tray, cut side up, dot in the unpeeled garlic and drizzle with olive oil. Season with salt and pepper and scatter over the oregano. Place the tray in the oven and slowly cook the tomatoes for 1–1½ hours, so they cook down and become jammy – but not completely dried out. Scatter the pine nuts in a smaller tray and add to the oven for the last 12 minutes of cooking, just to toast them slightly.

While the tomatoes are cooling, cook the orzo. Place a large pan of salted water on to boil, cook the pasta according to the packet instructions until just cooked through, then drain, reserving a mug of the hot, starchy pasta water. Rinse the pasta in a fine colander or sieve under cold running water, to stop it overcooking and cool it quickly, then drain and transfer to a large mixing bowl.

To make the dressing, carefully remove the garlic from the tomato tray and pop the flesh from the skins. Place the garlic flesh in a mixing bowl, then use the back of a fork to mash the soft garlic with a pinch of salt and the red wine vinegar. Once they are smooth, whisk in the mustard, extra virgin olive oil and add a generous couple of pinches of pepper. Toss the dressing into the pasta along with the cooked, cooled tomatoes and toasted pine nuts.. If it doesn't quite feel loose enough, add a splash of pasta water. Tear in all the basil leaves, add the rocket and mix together well. Serve straight away or keep in the fridge until needed. If you are making ahead of time, leave the torn basil leaves and rocket in a layer on top of the dressed pasta and mix together at the last minute.

Pomegranate fattoush

As a kid I could never understand why the adults in my family would fight over the salad bowl, dunking their bread into the juices at the bottom... I came to see the error of my ways and now know there are few things better than bread saturated in a tangy, punchy salad dressing. Fattoush is one of my favourite salads – it's the perfect vehicle for slightly stale pita bread (the Arabic word '*fatteh*' means 'crumbs') given a new lease of life in crunchy, peppery, sweet salad. I've ramped up the tart and sweet elements with pomegranate, and I think it works a dream.

SERVES 4–6

2 pita breads
Extra virgin olive oil
1 teaspoon dried oregano
Sea salt and freshly ground black pepper
1 tablespoon pomegranate molasses
1 lemon
1 garlic clove
½ pomegranate
500g ripe, mixed-colour tomatoes
1 small or ½ large cucumber
6 spring onions
1 bunch of flat-leaf parsley
6 radishes
1 cos lettuce or 2 little gem lettuces
1 teaspoon sumac

Preheat the oven to 180°C/fan 160°C/gas mark 4. Open out the pita breads like a book and drizzle with olive oil, sprinkle over the oregano and season a little. Pop in the oven for 12–15 minutes until lightly golden and crisp. Leave to cool for 10 minutes, then break them up.

While the pita are in the oven, make the dressing. Whisk or shake together two tablespoons of extra virgin olive oil, the pomegranate molasses and the juice of the lemon. Peel and crush the garlic clove with the side of your knife and add it to the dressing. Season generously, whisk together then leave to one side. Pick the pomegranate seeds and keep to one side.

Roughly chop the tomatoes, trim and chop the cucumber (if you are using a large cucumber, halve it lengthways and scoop out the middle). Trim and finely slice the spring onions. Pick the parsley leaves and finely chop. Trim and finely slice the radishes. Trim and roughly chop the cos or little gem. Toss everything together with the dressing (discarding the garlic) and spread out onto a platter. Scatter over the toasted pita and the pomegranate seeds and sprinkle over the sumac, then serve.

Charred watermelon and pistachio

The weeks leading up to the assumption of the Blessed Virgin Mary in August is one of the biggest fasting periods in the Orthodox calendar, and I love the opportunity to really focus on and embrace the abundance of summer produce here. The idea of cooked watermelon takes most people by surprise, but grilling it adds a sweet and smoky caramelisation that pairs so well with a vibrant and nutty pesto dressing. I make this simple salad throughout the barbecue months, and when I'm not fasting I'll sometimes have it with a chunk of feta or some grilled meat.

SERVES 6

5 mint sprigs
½ bunch of basil
1 small garlic clove
50g pistachios
1 lemon
Extra virgin olive oil
Sea salt and freshly ground black pepper
1 green chilli
1kg watermelon

Pick the mint and basil leaves. Peel the garlic clove. Reserve a few mint and basil leaves, then put the rest of the herbs in a food processor with the garlic, pistachios, juice of the lemon, four tablespoons of extra virgin olive oil and a good pinch of salt and pepper and then pulse until you have a paste that still has a nice bit of coarse, nutty texture. Spoon over a large platter and don't worry if it feels a little thick, the watermelon will release a lot of liquid.

Halve, deseed and finely slice the chilli, then set aside. Slice the watermelon into 1.5cm-thick slices and cook on the barbecue for around 5 minutes on each side until charred. You can also do this in a hot griddle pan or large dry frying pan. Cut the grilled slices into wedges and place on top of the pistachio pesto. Drizzle with a little extra virgin olive and season. Scatter over the sliced chilli and the reserved mint and basil leaves and serve immediately.

(Photo overleaf)

Fennel, pear and almond salad

The first time I made this salad I ate the whole thing, all four portions, in one sitting. It doesn't have loads of punchy flavours but the gently spiced nuts and the crunchy, fresh green base make it quietly addictive. Serve it with heavy or creamy dishes that need something to cut through the richness. Or just eat it on its own. On your own...

SERVES 4

1 teaspoon fennel seeds
40g blanched almonds
½ teaspoon poppy seeds
Olive oil
Sea salt and freshly ground black pepper
1 fennel bulb
2 crunchy pears (or apples)
2 tablespoons apple cider vinegar
4 tablespoons extra virgin olive oil
80g rocket

Preheat the oven to 200°C/fan 180°C/gas mark 6. Crush the fennel seeds using a pestle and mortar or spice grinder. Roughly chop the almonds and toss with the crushed fennel seeds, poppy seeds, a little olive oil and season generously. Spread out on a small baking tray and toast in the oven for 8–10 minutes, until the almonds are golden. Remove and set aside to cool.

Trim the fennel bulb of any tough or discoloured bits. Cut the pears of apples into thin wedges, removing core as you go. In a large mixing bowl whisk together the apple cider vinegar and extra virgin olive oil with a good pinch of salt and pepper until combined. Place the fruit wedges on top and then shave in the fennel, using either a mandoline (carefully) or a potato peeler. Add the rocket and toss everything together. Spread out onto a serving plate, scatter over the cooled nuts and seeds and serve straight away.

(Photo overleaf)

Left to right: charred watermelon and pistachio (page 70); fennel, pear and almond salad (page 71); village-style tomatoes with crisp capers (page 74)

Village-style tomatoes with crisp capers

Tomatoes are one of the heroes in Greek cooking. They are the base of so many of our foods – stewed, baked, puréed, you'll even find them made into glyko, a sweet preserve. For me though, there is nothing quite like eating them straight up in a traditional Greek salad.

SERVES 4

600g ripe tomatoes (a mixture of sizes and colours if possible)
Sea salt and freshly ground black pepper
½ red onion
1 tablespoon red wine vinegar
3 tablespoons extra virgin olive oil
2 tablespoon capers
¼ teaspoon dried oregano

Slice and cut the tomatoes into various chunks, slices and wedges. Place in a colander directly into your sink (or over a mixing bowl) and toss a half-teaspoon of sea salt through the tomatoes. Leave the tomatoes in the colander for 20 minutes, but give them a shake every few minutes, so they release their excess liquid.

Meanwhile, peel and very finely slice the red onion. Place in a large serving bowl and scrunch together with the red wine vinegar and a pinch of salt, then set aside for 10 minutes. Pour one tablespoon of the oil into a small frying or saucepan. Place on a medium heat and fry the drained capers for 3–4 minutes, until they turn a little crisp. Remove from the heat.

When the tomatoes and red onions are ready, mix the remaining two tablespoons of olive oil into the onions. Add the tomatoes to the bowl, season with freshly ground black pepper and sprinkle over the dried oregano. Toss everything together and finish by spooning over the crisp capers and oil from the pan. Serve straight away.

(Photo on previous page)

Salatet malfouf: *a lip-puckering cabbage slaw*

Variations of salatet malfouf can be found throughout the Middle East and Cyprus (we call it *krambosalata*). Our family's recipe is incredibly simple, but I love the variety of vegetables in the Lebanese versions – peppery radishes, crunchy cucumber, you even find some with tomatoes. What they all share is a lip-puckeringly tangy, salty dressing that's punchy enough to almost wilt the ingredients and take the edge off the raw onion.

SERVES 6–8

½ white cabbage, about 500g
1 onion
8 radishes
1 cucumber
½ bunch of flat-leaf parsley
2 lemons
4 tablespoons extra virgin olive oil
Sea salt and freshly ground black pepper
½ tablespoon za'atar (page 111)

Trim the cabbage, remove the core and shred the leaves as finely as you can. Peel, halve and slice the onion just as finely. Trim and finely slice the radishes and cucumber. Finely chop the parsley, stalks and leaves. Squeeze the juice of one and a half lemons into a large mixing bowl and whisk in the extra virgin olive oil till it starts to emulsify, and season generously. Add the finely sliced cabbage and onion, and really scrunch in the dressing. Leave it for 10 minutes, then stir in the sliced radishes, cucumber and chopped parsley. Toss together, and give it a taste.
It should be lip-puckeringly lemony, so add more lemon juice as needed and adjust the seasoning. Finish by sprinkling over the za'atar. Unlike most salads, salatet malfouf is even nicer once it has sat for a while, so if you have time, leave it to one side for half an hour before serving.

Cooked root vegetable slaw, an addiction

I love a fresh crunchy slaw as much as the next person, but this Russian-inspired slaw occupies a place on my mental list of 'favourite book recipes', and declaring my addiction in the recipe title makes it official. Glossy, sweet and still earthy, this is everything I want from a side dish. Make a large batch and keep it in your fridge for several days – a spoonful will pep up any simple meal.

SERVES 6–8

500g beetroot
200g carrots
2 onions
2 garlic cloves
300g tomatoes
100ml sunflower oil
50ml wine vinegar (red or white is fine)
60g granulated sugar
Sea salt and freshly ground black pepper
½ bunch of dill

Trim, peel and coarsely grate the beetroot and carrots. This is easiest done in a food processor with a grating attachment. However, if you don't have one you can use a box grater – be prepared for some serious hand stains (consider wearing gloves)! Peel and finely chop the onions and garlic – if you're using a food processor, you can grate these also. Peel the tomatoes (see page 287) then finely chop them. Place the sunflower oil, wine vinegar and sugar in a large saucepan on a high heat, then add all the grated and chopped vegetables and season generously. Bring to the boil, then reduce to a simmer and cover the pan. Cook for 1½–2 hours, stirring occasionally, until the vegetables are tender. Remove the lid, raise the heat a little and cook for a further 15 minutes, until almost all the liquid has cooked away and the vegetables are soft and look glossy. Remove from the heat and leave to cool. Taste, tweak the seasoning and finely chop the dill. Stir through the dill before serving.

Wild mushroom, cherry and buckwheat salad

This salad is my riff on *kasha*, the name given to toasted buckwheat groats cooked (in water or milk) throughout Russia and Ukraine. The word *kasha* basically translates as 'porridge' but although in the west we think of porridge as a breakfast food, *kasha* is commonly a comforting, hearty, savoury dish or side at lunch or dinner – often far less liquid and overcooked than oat porridge. By all means you can serve this salad hot, but I especially like it served at room temperature. The key really is toasting the buckwheat first – it brings out an extra nutty flavour and also stops it all from being too mushy.

SERVES 4–6

Sunflower oil
225g buckwheat
450ml hot vegetable stock
Sea salt and freshly ground black pepper
800g mixed wild mushrooms
4 garlic cloves
1–2 teaspoons pul biber, or dried chilli flakes
1 bunch of spring onions
½ bunch of dill
1 bunch of flat-leaf parsley
2 lemons
80g dried cherries

Drizzle a little sunflower oil into a large frying pan and toast the buckwheat over a medium heat for 4–5 minutes, until it smells nutty and starts taking on a more golden hue. Spoon the buckwheat into a medium saucepan, pour in the vegetable stock and bring to the boil. Season then cover and reduce the heat a little. Cook for 15 minutes, or until the buckwheat is just tender. Check it a little before and keep an eye on it, otherwise it will turn to mush. When it is ready, remove from the heat. Fork the buckwheat out onto a large plate to cool quickly, so that it doesn't overcook.

While the buckwheat is cooling, fry the mushrooms. Wipe and trim them. Slice any large ones and leave any nice-looking or exotic ones whole. Peel and finely chop the garlic. Place the large frying pan you toasted the buckwheat in on a medium heat and drizzle in a couple of tablespoons of sunflower oil. Fry the mushrooms for 12–15 minutes, so that they release all their liquid then start to crisp up and turn golden. Add the chopped garlic halfway through, with one teaspoon of pul biber, and generous pinches of salt and pepper (I think it needs at least one teaspoon of flaky sea salt). When the mushrooms are ready, remove the pan from the heat and leave to one side.

Trim and finely slice the spring onions. Pick and roughly chop the dill and parsley leaves. Add them all to a mixing bowl and toss with the cooled buckwheat and fried mushrooms. Squeeze over the juice of both lemons and stir in the dried cherries. Mix everything together, taste and tweak the seasoning, then serve.

Griddled red chicory, spelt and pomegranate

This recipe is a go-to of mine when fasting during the winter months. Spring and summer fasting periods are often easier – there's an abundance of fresh produce to play with, and I often want to eat lighter food. A grain-based salad is perfect for cooler, shorter days. Chicory is robust enough to withstand grilling, or even pan-frying, which lends it a nutty flavour that really goes well with grains, in this case spelt. Being a slightly bitter leaf, it goes well with sweeter dressings, and pomegranate is the perfect pairing.

SERVES 4

Sea salt and freshly ground black pepper
150g spelt
Extra virgin olive oil
2 shallots
1 pomegranate
½ bunch of flat-leaf parsley
40g walnuts
2 red chicory
3 tablespoons olive oil
1 teaspoon Dijon mustard
2 tablespoons pomegranate molasses
1 tablespoon balsamic vinegar
1 bunch of basil

Place a large pan of salted water on to boil. Cook the spelt according to the packet instructions and then drain in a sieve. Spoon into a large serving bowl and stir in a little extra virgin olive oil. While the spelt is cooking, get on with the rest of the salad. Peel and finely slice the shallots. Carefully pick the pomegranate seeds from the fruit. Pick and chop the parsley leaves.

Place a large frying pan on a medium heat and toast the walnuts until lightly golden, then transfer to a board and leave to cool. Trim the chicory, slice into quarters, then slice each wedge in half so you end up with thin wedges. Wipe the frying pan clean, drizzle in one tablespoon of olive oil and fry the chicory on a high heat until lightly browned at the edges. You don't want to sauté them, just cook them quickly to char them a little. Remove from the pan and keep to one side. Pour the remaining olive oil into the pan, add the sliced shallots and turn the heat down to soften. Slowly sauté for 10 minutes, then stir in the mustard, pomegranate molasses and balsamic vinegar. Remove from the heat.

Toss the charred chicory and hot dressing through the spelt along with the pomegranate seeds and chopped parsley. Tear in the basil leaves and season to taste. Chop the toasted walnuts and scatter over the top.

Sauerkraut and herb potato salad

When I was growing up, our potato salads and slaws were never mayonnaise-based, and I still find creamy dressings too rich if I am honest. However, this fresh, herby potato salad is almost a halfway point. It's mayonnaise- and sour cream-free, but the honey-mustard dressing becomes thick and even a little creamy when mixed with the sauerkraut and spuds.

SERVES 4–6

Sea salt and freshly ground black pepper
750g new potatoes
1 garlic clove
1 red onion
2 tablespoons red wine vinegar or cider vinegar
3 tablespoons extra virgin olive oil
1 heaped teaspoon Dijon mustard
2 teaspoons honey (or agave)
100g sauerkraut
½ teaspoon caraway seeds
½ bunch of dill
A few mint or tarragon sprigs

Bring a large pan of salted water to the boil. Halve and quarter the potatoes, so that they are all a similar size, and place in the pan. Cook for around 15 minutes, until tender. Drain well, and leave to steam dry for 5 minutes.

Meanwhile, peel and finely chop the garlic and red onion. Place in a large mixing bowl with the vinegar and half a teaspoon each of sea salt and freshly ground black pepper. Leave for 5 minutes, then whisk in the extra virgin olive oil, Dijon mustard and honey. Roughly chop the sauerkraut and crush the caraway seeds, and add both to the bowl. Pick the dill and mint or tarragon leaves, finely chop and leave to one side.

When the potatoes are cooked and have steamed dry but are still hot, stir into the dressing. Leave to cool completely, stirring occasionally. Taste and adjust the seasoning. Then when the potatoes have cooled, stir in the chopped fresh herbs and serve.

Roast beetroot, lentils and walnuts

This recipe doesn't have a specific origin but there are definitely influences from Eastern Europe. It's a balance of complementary flavours and one of my favourite ways to eat beetroot. If you can find golden or candy-striped beets, even better as their sweetness works perfectly.

SERVES 4–6

- 600g beetroot, mixed colours if possible
- 4 red onions
- 4 garlic cloves
- Olive oil
- Sea salt and freshly ground black pepper
- 1 teaspoon caraway seeds
- 40g walnuts
- 150g green or puy lentils
- 3 tablespoons red wine vinegar
- 1 teaspoon Dijon mustard
- 1 teaspoon honey (or maple syrup)
- 3 tablespoons extra virgin olive oil
- ½ bunch of flat-leaf parsley
- ½ bunch of mint
- 50g wild rocket

Preheat your oven to 200°C/fan 180°C/gas mark 6. Peel the beetroot and cut into 2–3cm chunks and wedges. Peel and cut the onions into similar sized wedges. Crush the garlic in its skin. Place all the vegetables in a roasting tray and drizzle with olive oil, season well and scatter over the caraway seeds. Toss together and place in the oven for around 50–60 minutes, until caramelised on the edges and the beetroot is cooked through. Place the walnuts in a small tray and toast them in the oven for the last 5 minutes, so they become lightly golden. Remove the two trays from the oven and leave to cool for at least 10 minutes.

Meanwhile, cook the lentils. Give them a rinse in a sieve then place in a pan and add enough cold water to cover by a few centimetres. Bring to the boil, then simmer for 18–20 minutes, until tender but not mushy. Drain the cooked lentils thoroughly. In a large serving bowl, mix the red wine vinegar with the Dijon mustard, honey and extra virgin olive oil, and season. Whisk together then stir in the drained lentils. When the vegetables are ready, toss them through the lentils also. Roughly chop the walnuts. Pick and roughly chop the herb leaves and add them, the walnuts and rocket to the salad just before serving, ideally at room temperature.

Green tabbouleh

Traditional tabbouleh is made with fine bulgur wheat, which you don't have to precook – soaking and dressing it alone is enough. However, if you are unable to get hold of this, use regular bulgur wheat and cook according to the packet instructions. Leave to drain and cool thoroughly before using. Alternatively, you can grind regular uncooked bulgur wheat in a food processor, so it is finer, then follow the recipe as instructed. Unlike most salads, tabbouleh is better made a little ahead of time. It can be left covered in the fridge for several hours, even overnight, if needed.

SERVES 6

5 spring onions
2 Greek or Lebanese cucumbers or 1 large English cucumber
2 large bunches of flat-leaf parsley
1 bunch of mint
15 green olives
75g fine bulgur wheat
1 avocado (not too ripe)
2 lemons
Sea salt and freshly ground black pepper
4 tablespoons extra virgin olive oil
1 romaine or cos lettuce, optional

Trim and finely chop the spring onions and cucumbers. Trim the parsley stalks, and pick the mint leaves, and chop everything together until very fine. Remove and discard the stones from the olives, and finely chop the flesh. Place everything in a large mixing bowl.

Place the fine bulgur wheat in a bowl and cover with cold water. Leave to soak for 10 minutes, then drain in a sieve and dry on kitchen paper. You don't want any water in the salad. Peel, destone and finely chop the avocado. Add both to the mixing bowl with the chopped herb mixture and squeeze over the juice from both lemons. Season generously with salt and pepper and drizzle over the extra virgin olive oil. Toss everything together well, then cover and leave in the fridge for at least 30 minutes, or longer, until needed. Serve the tabbouleh as is, or, in lettuce boats. Trim the romaine or cos lettuce, click the leaves apart and wash and dry well. Then fill with the dressed tabbouleh and serve.

(Photo overleaf)

Roasted garlic muhammara

Originally from Syria, muhammara is made and eaten throughout the Levant. You don't have to roast the garlic first, but it adds a depth of flavour and sweetness that I love – it's worth roasting more cloves than you'll need here and storing them in olive oil to use in other dips and dressings. If you prefer to use raw garlic, you'll only need one or two cloves so as not to overpower the other ingredients. As with a lot of dips and sauces, the flavours of muhammara really develop over time, so make it the day before you want to serve it, store in the fridge overnight, then leave to come to room temperature before serving.

If you did want to make this a very quick dip, then using ready-roasted, jarred red peppers is not the end of the world. Look, it's not the same, they lose some of that wonderful intense smokiness you get when grilling them from having been stored in a jar. But equally, it's OK, and I won't tell anyone. While we're talking changes: if you don't have a food processor and you want to make this with a hand blender, pestle and mortar, or a large, really sharp knife, you can. You'll have a few more logistical issues because of the ingredient quantities, but it will work out.

SERVES 6–8

4 garlic cloves
Extra virgin olive oil
50g walnuts
¾ teaspoon cumin seeds
4 large red peppers
1 red chilli
Sea salt and freshly ground black pepper
75g white breadcrumbs
4 tablespoons pomegranate molasses
½ lemon
A few pinches of pul biber
A few mint sprigs

Preheat your oven to 180°C/fan 160°C/gas mark 4. Place the garlic cloves in a small dish (that will also eventually fit the walnuts) and rub them with a little olive oil. Pop in the oven and cook for 20 minutes. Remove the tray, scatter in the walnuts and cumin seeds and return to the oven for 8 minutes, or until the walnuts are golden. Leave to one side to cool. Meanwhile, place the peppers and chilli on an open flame (over your hob or a barbecue) and cook them, turning often so they char evenly. When charred all over, put them in a bowl and cover with cling film. When they are cool enough to handle, peel and discard the skin and seeds. Roughly chop the flesh.

When everything is cool, make the muhammara. Peel the garlic cloves and add to the bowl of a food processor along with the walnuts and cumin seeds. Blitz until roughly chopped. Add the peeled and chopped peppers and chilli and season well. Pulse until everything is just finely chopped together, but you don't have a sloppy paste. Pulse in the breadcrumbs, two tablespoons of the pomegranate molasses and the juice of the lemon half. When it is all combined, stir in enough extra virgin olive oil to loosen the mixture, and have a taste. Tweak the seasoning, then spoon onto a serving plate. Drizzle with the remaining molasses, a little more oil and sprinkle over the pul biber. Pick and roughly chop the mint leaves and sprinkle over before serving.

(Photo overleaf)

Clockwise from top left: roasted garlic muhammara (page 87); Maroulla's spiced courgettes (page 134); tsakistes (page 91); arnabeet (page 135); classic houmous (page 90); green tabbouleh (page 86)

Classic houmous

However you spell it, there is no denying that houmous preferences are a personal thing, and everyone has their own way of making it. At the risk of offending my people, I admit that I far prefer the smooth, moussey Middle Eastern form to the coarser, more rustic kind you find in Cyprus. The secret to this light texture is to blitz the chickpeas with some of the water they were cooked in. (Chickpea water is sometimes called aquafaba, and used as an egg replacement in many vegan recipes, due to its resemblance in texture when whipped to egg white.)

If you can, cook your own chickpeas and peel them, too – I think you can really taste the difference. However, if time is against you, I have also included instructions for how to use jarred ones (you can pick up lovely ones inexpensively from good international grocers). If you do have to use tinned, please, *please* use good-quality, organic chickpeas.

SERVES 8–12

500g cooked chickpeas (see page 289) or 500g jarred/tinned chickpeas (drained weight, liquid reserved)
2 garlic cloves
1–2 lemons
100g tahini
Sea salt
Extra virgin olive oil
Paprika, for sprinkling

When you have cooked your chickpeas according to the method on page 289, leave them in their cooking liquor to cool down. Peeling them here makes all the difference to the end texture.

Whether you're using cooked dried chickpeas or jarred/tinned ones, drain them in a colander, but keep the liquid. Peel the garlic cloves, then finely grate them into a food processor and squeeze in the juice of 1 lemon. Add the tahini and a good splash of the chickpea water and blitz till you have a pale, loose paste. Add the drained chickpeas and a generous pinch of salt and blitz until creamy. Taste and add more salt and lemon juice. If it feels a little thick and grainy, add a small splash of chickpea water (not too much or you could end up with a sloppy mess; you can always add a little more). When the houmous has the flavour and texture you like, spoon it on to a serving plate, then drizzle with extra virgin olive oil and sprinkle with paprika.

(Photo on previous page)

Tsakistes: *lemon and coriander marinated olives*

One of those most evocative smells for me is of tsakistes – young green olives that are cracked then marinated in garlic, lemon and coriander seeds. My yiayia and mum will often have a little bowl of them out on their kitchen counters, and even with a side plate covering the bowl the smell is intoxicating enough to fill the kitchen. Finding the young green olives needed to make this can be challenging – they're only available during September and October and you'll need to find a Greek or Turkish greengrocer who stocks them. Each olive then needs to be cracked with a stone (or pestle), then soaked in a large vat of cold water. The water is changed every day for seven to ten days, to get rid of the bitterness, before the olives are brined for three weeks. Only then can you marinate them with the ingredients below.

Alternatively, you can use the same marinade to enhance regular green olives. Pick the smallest ones possible; if they're the big fat ones, the flavours won't penetrate as well.

SERVES MANY

500g small green olives (either fresh or in brine)
50ml extra virgin olive oil
2 lemons
3 garlic cloves
2 teaspoons coriander seeds
Sea salt

To serve: A few fresh coriander sprigs and a few pinches of pul biber or dried chilli flakes

If you are using the fresh young green olives, prepare them as instructed in the introduction. Alternatively just drain the preserved ones and place them in a bowl. Stir in the extra virgin olive oil and squeeze in the juice of half of one of the lemons. Cut the remaining lemon half into two, then slice into 1cm half-moon slices. Crush the garlic with the flat of your knife, remove the skin and stir the cloves into the olives with the lemon slices. Crush the coriander seeds – doesn't need to be too fine, crushed and halved is fine – and add to the bowl also. Stir all together, taste and season with salt to taste and add more lemon juice if needed. You can serve immediately, or ideally leave for a few days so the olives really take on all the flavours. If that is the case, store the olives covered in the fridge, then leave at room temperature for a few hours before serving.

I like to serve mine with finely chopped fresh coriander stirred through, and sprinkled with a pinch of pul biber or chilli flakes.

(Photo on previous page)

Baka Mara's meljanac: *crushed beans with paprika and garlic*

Kristina Vučinić taught me so many new things about Serbian fasting food for this book, but when she described this recipe I started laughing in recognition. Her *baka* (grandmother) Mara always insisted on using a lot of oil with these beans. It's always been the same with both my yiayias, using so much oil that it dismays their children. But grandmothers are older and wiser, and they know that fat equals flavour, especially in such a simple dish. 'If you get scared of oil, these will never taste like my grandmother's beans, they will be more like my mum's beans,' Kristina told me. 'Also, when serving, my grandmother always drizzles this with extra oil, to my mum's horror, but those are the rules.' I will not argue with Baka Mara's rules.

SERVES 4–6

200g dried cannellini beans or 2 × 400g jars/tins of beans
1 carrot
1 onion
3 bay leaves
A few black peppercorns
Sea salt
8 tablespoons sunflower oil
1 tablespoon plain flour
1 heaped teaspoon sweet paprika
2 garlic cloves

Soak the dried beans overnight in plenty of cold water.

The next day, drain the beans and add them to a medium-sized saucepan and cover with fresh water. Peel and roughly chop the carrot and half the onion and add to the pan with the bay leaves and peppercorns. Bring to the boil on a high heat, then reduce the heat to medium-low and simmer gently for 1–1½ hours, or until the beans are tender. When the beans are cooked, drain them in a colander and take out the vegetables, bay leaves and peppercorns. If you're using tinned or jarred beans, drain them, then start from here. Return the beans to the saucepan and use a potato masher to crush them into a paste. This should be quite smooth, but not smushed to a fine purée. Season with salt to taste.

Peel and finely chop the remaining onion half. Add four tablespoons of the oil to a medium frying pan; ideally, you want at least 5mm covering the base of your pan. Place the pan over a medium-low heat and gently fry the chopped onion for around 10 minutes so that it softens and turns only very lightly golden. Quickly stir in the plain flour and paprika until you have a paste then remove from the heat, as burning the onions and paprika will make it bitter. Pour the roux over the mashed beans and mix in well. Taste and adjust the seasoning as needed, then spoon the beans into a serving dish. Wipe out the frying pan with kitchen paper, then return to the hob and add four more tablespoons of oil. Peel and finely slice the garlic cloves and add to the pan. Fry them gently on a low heat, then when they're just turning golden pour the garlic and the infused oil over the crushed beans. Serve straight away – I like this on toast, or just with a pile of toasted flatbread or pita for scooping it up.

Tashi, teradot, toum: *a tale of three garlic sauces*

Any one of these sauces would make a welcome addition to any meze or plate. Tashi makes an appearance in most feast situations for my Cypriot family – including our Christmas dinner! Turkish teradot and toum from Lebanon would have the same impact – creamy and moreish, yet so punchy with garlic that it's worth remembering a little goes a long way.

Tashi

SERVES 6

150g tahini
1–2 garlic cloves
1 lemon
2 tablespoons extra virgin olive oil
Sea salt and freshly ground white pepper
A few flat-leaf parsley sprigs, optional

Spoon the tahini into a mixing bowl. Peel and finely grate in the garlic clove (adding another if you like your sauces quite punchy). Whisk together, then slowly pour in 160ml of just-boiled water, whisking it in the whole time until smooth. You will end up with a pale, thick dip. Squeeze in the juice of the lemon, and add a tablespoon of the extra virgin olive oil. Mix in and season to taste. Place the tashi in the fridge for at least 1 hour, to thicken slightly. Serve drizzled with the remaining extra virgin olive oil, and a sprinkle of chopped parsley, if you like.

Teradot

If you have any roasted garlic, that would be a pleasant swap to the raw used here, especially if you like a milder, slightly sweet sauce.

SERVES 6–8

2 garlic cloves (or 3 roasted cloves)
125g walnuts
Sea salt and freshly ground black pepper
3 tablespoons tahini
2 lemons
1 large bunch of flat-leaf parsley
Extra virgin olive oil

Peel and finely chop the garlic, then add to the bowl of a food processor with the walnuts, plus a quarter-teaspoon each of sea salt and freshly ground black pepper. Blitz until very finely ground. Add the tahini to the bowl and pulse in until you have a paste. Scoop the mixture into a bowl and stir in the juice of both the lemons and four tablespoons of boiling water. Mix together well, until you have a creamy sauce. Taste and adjust the seasoning. Pick and very finely chop the flat-leaf parsley leaves and stir into the sauce. Garnish with a drizzle of extra virgin olive oil and a few sprigs of parsley, if you have some left.

Toum

Toum is found throughout the Levant, and is served much in the same way as *alioli* in Spain – alongside chips, or with grilled meats or seafood. While there are no eggs in toum, it needs to be handled in the same way – made slowly so it emulsifies and so that the mixture does not split. You can make this in a mini food processor or with a large pestle and mortar; if using the latter, it will be easier if you halve the ingredients below so they fit in the mortar – and get prepared to employ a bit of elbow grease.

SERVES 6–8

1 head of garlic
1 teaspoon sea salt
1 lemon
400ml vegetable or sunflower oil (or any flavourless oil)
3 ice cubes (or 3 tablespoons iced water)

Peel all the garlic cloves. If you're using a mini food processor, place all the garlic in the bowl and blitz along with the sea salt until very finely chopped. Then squeeze in the lemon juice (discarding the pips) and blitz in until you have a smooth paste.

If you are using a large pestle and mortar, halve the ingredients or make this in two batches. Roughly chop the garlic first then place in the mortar with the salt and bash until creamy and smooth. Pound in the lemon juice until you have a paste.

Whichever method you are using, the next step is key. Working slowly, either with the food processor motor running, or just making sure you take your time, blitz or pound the vegetable oil into the garlic paste.
If using the food processor, drizzle the oil into the opening on the top in a very slow and steady stream. After you have added about 150ml, add an ice cube to the bowl and blitz in. Repeat until you have used all the oil and ice cubes – this should take 10 minutes or so.

If making it by hand, follow the same instructions, working in thirds, but instead of an ice cube, use a tablespoon of iced water. The toum is ready when it is white, fluffy, light in texture and emulsified.

Apple, fennel and dill sauerkraut

This delicious recipe from Alissa Timoshkina's book *Salt and Time* was my first foray into making sauerkraut, and to this day is still one of my favourite ferments. If you are new to fermenting foods then this is a great starting point – it's easy and hugely rewarding. As Alissa recommends in her book: 'This sauerkraut can be consumed on its own with a little drizzle of good-quality unrefined sunflower oil, or add some blood oranges, jalapeños and dill to turn it into a delicious winter salad.'

MAKES ENOUGH FOR A 1-LITRE JAR

1 teaspoon fennel seeds
1 white cabbage, about 800g
1½ tablespoons fine sea salt
1 fennel bulb
1 Granny Smith apple
1 bunch of dill

Sterilise your jar (see page 287). Toast the fennel seeds in a small dry pan over a low heat for a couple of minutes, then leave to one side to cool. Remove the outer leaves from the cabbage, keeping one leaf aside for later, and cut the rest into quarters. Turn onto a cut edge, and finely slice using a sharp knife or mandolin. Place in a large mixing bowl with the sea salt, massage it all in and leave to one side to wilt slightly.

While the cabbage is being salted, trim the fennel bulb, slice in half and finely slice also. Halve, remove the core from the apple and finely slice also. Roughly chop the dill. Add it all to the bowl with the cabbage, plus the toasted fennel seeds, and mix together – you should notice liquid in the bottom of the bowl. Mix and massage it all together for 5 minutes, to ensure more juices are released.

Pack the mixture into your jar, layering it up and pressing down with your fist as you go so there are no pockets of air. By this point the cabbage should have released enough of its own liquid to be fully submerged in its own juices. When you are finished, place the reserved leaf over the top, and something heavy to weight down the mixture, like a small ramekin. Close the jar tightly and leave to ferment out of direct sunlight at room temperature for 10–14 days, opening to release the gases every other day. Taste the cabbage after 10 days and leave to ferment for longer if needed. Once you are happy with the taste, transfer the jar to the fridge to slow down the fermentation process. It will keep in the cold for up to 6 months.

Ajvar

This Serbian condiment has semi-permanent residence in my fridge as it can instantly transform even the simplest of meals – roasted cauliflower, flatbreads or (if you eat them) an omelette or grilled fish. It isn't a million miles away from the Romanian *zacusca*, which has the addition of tomatoes. So if you want to bulk this recipe out, or tone down the fierce garlic, you simply blitz fresh, peeled tomatoes into the mix before cooking at the end.

MAKES 8–10 SERVINGS

2 aubergines
4 red peppers
3 garlic cloves
Sea salt and freshly ground black pepper
5 tablespoons extra virgin olive oil, plus extra to serve
½ tablespoon red or white wine vinegar
½ teaspoon dried chilli flakes, optional, plus extra to serve

You can cook the vegetables under the grill or, if you'd rather, in the oven. I prefer the flavour under the grill, but the oven is less time consuming. For the grill, preheat it to medium-high heat, and if cooking in the oven preheat it to its highest setting.

Pierce the aubergines all over with a sharp knife. Place under the grill with the red peppers and grill for around 30–40 minutes, turning several times, until blackened all over. If roasting in the oven, place the veg directly on the oven bars and roast for 20–30 minutes, until blackened. When they are all ready, place the red peppers in a bowl and cover with cling film. Leave for 10 minutes and then peel off the pepper skins. Roughly chop the flesh, discarding the stalk and seeds. Leave the aubergine to cool slightly. When it is cool enough to handle, remove the top, scoop out the flesh and discard the skin. Peel and chop the garlic. Blitz all the vegetables in a food processor and until finely chopped and creamy looking. Add half a teaspoon each of salt and pepper, the extra virgin olive oil, vinegar and chilli (if using) and blitz again. Spoon the mixture into a pan and gently cook gently over a low heat for 30–40 minutes, to thicken up. Leave to cool completely before serving. Serve with a drizzle of extra virgin olive oil and the dried chilli on top.

(Photo overleaf)

Marinated wild mushrooms

This concept isn't exclusive to one country, however this recipe is the way my yiayia taught me to preserve mushrooms and will be familiar to many (with variations on herbs and spices depending on where you are, I am sure). I make a vat of this in the autumn when mushrooms are at their best. Serve as part of a feast, on the side of a hearty rich meal, or as part of a meze.

SERVES MANY

1kg wild, or mixed, mushrooms
4 garlic cloves
175ml olive oil
100ml red wine vinegar
1 tablespoon coriander seeds
4 oregano sprigs or ½ teaspoon dried oregano
¼ teaspoon chilli flakes or pul biber
2 bay leaves
1 teaspoon peppercorns
1 teaspoon sea salt

Start by sterilising one large or two medium jars, as directed on page 287; if you plan on eating them straight away or over a few days, you can just keep this in an airtight container in the fridge. Next prepare the mushrooms. Wipe them clean, trim the ends and halve or quarter any larger ones. If you are using very large mushrooms, then slice them into 2cm-thick slices. Crush the garlic, in its skin, with the side of your knife, then add it to a large saucepan with the olive oil. Place on a medium-low heat and fry the whole cloves for 2–3 minutes, until you can start to smell them. Add all the remaining ingredients apart from the prepared mushrooms, and turn the heat up. Bring to the boil, then add the mushrooms. Cook for 6 minutes, then remove from the heat. Ladle straight into the sterilised jars – try to evenly distribute the aromatics if possible – then seal the jars while still hot. Leave to cool, and store in a dark cupboard. Once opened, transfer the jar to the fridge.

(Photo overleaf)

Kapari: *pickled caper stalks*

Pickled and salted tiny caper berries are easy to come by in the UK, and are readily sold in larger supermarkets and delis. However, I am yet to see pickled caper stalks anywhere other than a Cypriot person's home. They are a quintessential Cypriot preserve, and a wonderful accompaniment to any large meal. We often have a few sprigs of kapari on the side of dishes such as yiahni (page 125) or fasoles (page 186) – any of the richer, slow-cooked dishes.

To make kapari, caper stalks are gathered in either spring or summer when they are most tender, and placed into large glass or terracotta jars. They are submerged in cold water and left for 10 days, with the water being changed daily. After the soaking process, they are drained and coated in plenty of salt. The stalks are left out in the sun to dry thoroughly before being packed into sterilised glass jars. Finally, vinegar is poured into the jars until the caper stalks are fully covered and then the jars are sealed. Ideally they are left for a couple of months before eating, and will keep for a forgiving amount of time in a dark cool spot. You'll often find kapari served simply laid on a dish and drizzled with extra virgin olive oil, alongside stews and larger meals.

Left to right: kapari (opposite); avjar (page 98); moungra (page 102–3); marinated wild mushrooms (page 99)

Moungra: *fermented cauliflower in mustard seeds*

My paternal yiayia had been trying to teach me how to make moungra for years, as it is traditional to the region of Cyprus where she is from, but my young and untrained palate just wasn't on board. I wanted to learn a million other family recipes before she showed me how to ferment cauliflower in yeasted water. However, she persevered and I'm glad she did as I now love it; it is subtle, unusual and also – in terms of this book – apt. While moungra is made and eaten all year round it is actually meant to be made in the lead up to Great Lent and enjoyed on *Kathara Deftera* – Clean Monday (see page 19). If you have a good baker near you, ask them if you can buy some levain – they may even give you some for free.

MAKES 1 VERY LARGE JAR

1 × 7g sachet of fast-action dried yeast
100g strong white bread flour
1½ tablespoons fine sea salt

or 300g levain

1kg cauliflower
Ice
2 tablespoons yellow mustard seeds

To serve: Extra virgin olive oil

You will need a very large preserving jar for this – traditionally it would be made in a large crock or something similar. Mix the yeast into 200ml warm water and leave to one side. Mix the flour with a half-tablespoon of the salt in a large mixing bowl and then whisk in the yeast water until completely smooth. Cover the bowl with cling film and leave in a cool dark place for 3–4 days to ferment. (If using levain you can skip this step).

When ready to make the moungra, prepare the cauliflower. Remove any leaves and cut into florets, discarding the main large piece of stem – you should have around 700g of cauliflower at this stage. Place the florets in a bowl of iced water for 15 minutes. Bring a large pan of salted water to the boil. Using a slotted spoon, place the cauliflower florets into the boiling water for 2 minutes, then spoon them out and place back into the iced water. Once they are all cooked and cool, drain and leave to dry on a tea towel. Meanwhile, place 1 litre of water to boil. Slowly whisk the boiling water into the levain or yeast-flour mixture, until smooth and milky. Crush the mustard seeds in a pestle and mortar. You don't have to finely grind them, just crush.

To assemble the moungra, sterilise your large jar or crock (see page 287). Sprinkle some of the mustard seeds into the base, then add a layer of the blanched and dried cauliflower florets, then a sprinkling of sea salt. Repeat until the pot or jar is full, or you have used up all the ingredients. Carefully ladle in the yeast or sourdough water (using a funnel if you have one) until all the cauliflower is covered. Place the lid on and leave the pot in a cool dark spot for 8–10 days, turning the jar every day, and giving it a little shake. If you are using a crock, cover with a greaseproof lid, and put your (clean) hand in every day and turn the florets individually.

Taste the cauliflower; it should taste slightly sour and salty. Serve in a small bowl, drizzled with a little extra virgin olive oil on top. Store any extra moungra in the fridge to slow down the fermentation process. It will keep there for a good few months.

(Photo on previous page)

Spiced snacking nuts and seeds

Snacking on nuts and seeds is such a common sight around the eastern Mediterranean and Middle East, where both are served still in the shells, the shelling process being part of the enjoyment. I do like to pep mine up with seasoning and spices – the way you would buy already roasted and flavoured nuts in pubs and shops. This way I can balance them to my taste: punchy, salty, sweet, spicy... and very addictive.

SERVES MANY

¼ teaspoon black peppercorns
1 teaspoon nigella seeds
1 teaspoon aniseed or fennel seeds
1 teaspoon cumin seeds
¼ teaspoon sweet paprika
60g caster sugar
1–2 teaspoons sea salt (1 teaspoon if fine, 2 teaspoons if flaky)
1 tablespoon olive oil
200g shelled nuts, a mixture
50g mixed seeds

Preheat your oven to 200°C/fan 180°C/gas mark 6. Line a baking tray with greaseproof paper. Place the black peppercorns, nigella seeds, aniseed and cumin seeds in a mortar and crush with a pestle until ground but still with a little texture – do not let the mixture get too fine. Place the mixture in a small saucepan with the paprika, sugar, sea salt, olive oil and 50ml of water. Bring to the boil on a medium heat, then add all the nuts and seeds, give it a good stir and cook for a further 2–3 minutes until glossy.

Spoon the coated nuts onto the baking tray, making sure they are in one layer, then pop into the oven for 8–10 minutes, stirring halfway through. Leave to cool completely before eating, or store in an airtight container.

Spiced onion oil

A lot of pies in Greece and Cyprus cuisine are *nistisimo*, and they're great but the absence of butter can sometimes mean they lack that delicious flavour – and adding too much oil just makes them greasy. So I regularly make flavoured oils to give them an extra depth of flavour. This onion oil is inspired by a classic Chinese spring onion oil, which is a store-cupboard game changer, vamping up boiled noodles and rice in an instant. Slowly confiting the onions and leek gives a depth and sweetness to this oil, which the spices and sugar round out. I use this to glaze pies, but also to drizzle over grilled or roasted vegetables, or to dress any potatoes or grain – it is hugely versatile.

SERVES 12

2 bunches of spring onions
1 leek
400ml vegetable oil
2 tablespoons baharat (see page 110 for how to make your own)
1 heaped tablespoon caster sugar
1 teaspoon sea salt

Trim the spring onions then slice into 2cm lengths. Trim and finely slice the green part of the leek. Slice the white section into 1cm rings, then place all the leek in a colander and rinse thoroughly under cold running water to get rid of any dirt, then shake off and leave to dry on a clean tea towel. Place all the sliced alliums in a saucepan with the vegetable oil and put on a medium-low heat. You don't want to cook the onions and leeks too fast, rather infuse the oil and let them gently turn a very light golden colour. This should take around 15–20 minutes. When they are ready, stir in the baharat, caster sugar and salt and reduce the heat to low. Cook for a further 3 minutes. Remove the pan from the heat and leave to cool. Store in an airtight container or jar in the fridge and spoon out as and when needed.

Ladolemono: *lemon, oregano and olive oil dressing*

I have published a recipe for ladolemono before, but it is such a key part of Greek cooking that it feels mad not to feature it in some form here. The only difference in this recipe is the garlic. While I am fasting, I find I appreciate super-charged flavours so the addition of raw garlic is a must. Have a jar of this dressing in your fridge for using on everything from salads, to vegetables, grills and drizzling over bread.

MAKES ABOUT 150–200ML

3 lemons
1 garlic clove
100ml extra virgin olive oil
½ teaspoon dried oregano
Sea salt and freshly ground black pepper

Squeeze the lemons into a mixing bowl and discard the pips. You ideally want three or four tablespoons of juice. Peel the garlic clove, and crush it with the flat side of your knife. Add it to the bowl with the extra virgin olive oil, the dried oregano and a generous pinch each of sea salt and freshly ground black pepper. Whisk it all together and have a taste – if you are using it for salad leaves then season it generously. Either using straight away or transfer to a jam jar, keeping in the garlic clove, seal and store in the fridge until needed.

Below: spiced onion oil
Top, centre: ladolemono

Dukkah

Despite only recently being able to find dukkah on spice shelves in UK shops, this traditional Egyptian seasoning has been around for centuries. Translated from Arabic, *dukkah* means 'to pound' and traditionally it is made by crushing and pounding the nuts and spices using a pestle and mortar, which is how many still make their dukkah. The amounts aren't set in stone and can be played with according to your taste – this is a guide and how I like to make mine. A mixture of nuts is good; ideally, half should be almonds and the rest could be pistachios, hazelnuts or walnuts. But try it out with whatever you have. It is worth making a large batch, as it is incredibly versatile and can be used in all sorts of ways. Serve fresh pita with small bowls of this and extra virgin olive oil to dip into; use it to finish dips such as houmous or muhammara; or sprinkle it on soups and salads. If you are not fasting, then it is particularly delicious scattered over eggs.

MAKES A SMALL JAR

150g nuts, a mix of types
1 teaspoon fennel seeds
2 tablespoons sesame seeds
2 tablespoons coriander seeds
1 tablespoon cumin seeds
1 teaspoon nigella seeds
¼ teaspoon cayenne pepper, optional
2 teaspoons flaky sea salt or 1 teaspoon fine sea salt
1 teaspoon coarsely ground black pepper

Place the nuts in a dry frying pan and toast over a medium heat for around 3–4 minutes, until golden and toasted all over. Place in the bowl of a food processor and leave to cool as you toast the spices. Place the fennel, sesame, coriander, cumin and nigella seeds in the pan and toast for just a couple of minutes until you can really smell them. Remove from the heat and leave in the pan for a minute while you pulse the nuts. Pulse a few times to roughly chop, then add the toasted seeds, along with the remaining ingredients and pulse until roughly chopped and well combined. Do not let this become too fine, or it will turn into a paste. Transfer to an airtight container.

Spices, left to right: baharat (page 110); Lebanese seven-spice (page 111); dukkah (opposite); za'atar (page 111)

Baharat, za'atar and Lebanese seven-spice

These are all spices I like to have in my arsenal, ready for sprinkling and to add flavour to vegetable and grain dishes. You can buy all of these in most supermarkets, but they're so easy to make, and you can adjust the balance to your taste.

(Photos on previous page)

Baharat

The word *baharat* literally translates as 'spices' in Arabic. It is the generic term for a spice blend, a bit like garam masala in India or ras el hanout in Morocco. There will be flavours that appear repeatedly; however, different countries, communities and families will have their own blends. As well as the spices below you may find sumac, saffron and even chilli in there. This is a good starting base, so have a play and tweak to your taste.

MAKES A SMALL JAR

15 green cardamom pods
1½ teaspoons black peppercorns
1 tablespoon cumin seeds
2 teaspoons coriander seeds
1 teaspoon ground cinnamon
¼ teaspoon ground cloves
1 tablespoon sweet paprika
½ nutmeg

Remove the seeds from the cardamom pods, and discard the husks. Place the seeds in a small dry pan with the peppercorns, cumin seeds and coriander seeds and toast over a low heat for a couple of minutes until fragrant. Remove from the pan and leave to cool. When they are ready, grind using a pestle and mortar until fine, then mix in the ground cinnamon, ground cloves and sweet paprika. Finely grate in the nutmeg and mix well. Store in an airtight container and use as needed.

Za'atar

Za'atar refers to the blend of herbs and spices below, but is also the name of a wild herb found throughout the Middle East that is often likened to wild thyme or oregano. Use this blend in recipes such as the little buns on page 30, or sprinkled over salads or dips.

MAKES A SMALL JAR

- 2 tablespoons sesame seeds
- 2 tablespoons dried wild thyme or oregano
- 2 tablespoons sumac
- 1 teaspoon flaked sea salt

Toast the sesame seeds in a large dry frying pan over a medium heat until very lightly golden, then leave to cool. When they're ready, mix in the dried herbs, sumac and salt and store in an airtight container.

Lebanese seven-spice

As with baharat, Lebanese seven-spice will vary from family to family, and doesn't always limit itself to just seven spices. You will find the addition of ginger and fenugreek in some variations. Have a play and customise a blend your liking – this is how I make mine (sometimes with a little ground ginger, too).

MAKES A SMALL JAR

- 1 tablespoon peppercorns
- 2 teaspoons cumin seeds
- 2 tablespoons coriander seeds
- 1 tablespoon ground allspice
- 1 tablespoon ground cinnamon
- ½ teaspoon ground cloves
- ½ nutmeg

Toast the peppercorns, cumin seeds and coriander seeds in a small dry frying pan over a low heat for a couple of minutes until fragrant. After a couple of minutes, remove from the heat, leave to cool then finely grind them. Stir in the remaining ground spices and finely grate in the nutmeg. Mix everything together and store in an airtight container until needed.

3 *Harvest – seasonal vegetables*

In this section, you will find showstopping pies and tarts, as well as much more simple recipes such as the sweetest, slow-cooked vegetables. Something that became apparent when researching the foods and recipes for this chapter are the variations of the same thing throughout the region. In Greece, vegetables that have been slow-cooked in oil with the addition of lemon or tomatoes are referred to as *ladera/lathera* (the word *lathi* means oil, so it literally translates 'with oil'). It is a popular and traditional way to serve whatever is abundant, and is a method used throughout the former Ottoman empire. It may be obvious, but when a vegetable is in season, there really isn't a better way to enjoy it. It is a great method for 'make ahead' dishes, as they are almost always eaten at room temperature (and taste better the next day).

Bećar paprikaš: *slow-cooked peppers*

Bećar is the word for bachelor in northern Serbia, and there are many tales as to how this dish got its name: it was something a single man could make easily after a night out; or perhaps it was a typical dinner of the men who used to tend fields of summer produce. However it came about, if you ever look at a recipe and dismiss it based on the simplicity of the ingredient list, then this is one of the best examples I can think of to show you how much can be achieved with careful cooking. These slow-cooked peppers are so intensely sweet, I guarantee they'll stop you in your tracks. You'll often find different proteins cooked amongst the peppers – pork being a popular choice, chicken and eggs, too – but during times of fasting they are cooked straight up. And to be honest, you don't miss the meat at all. This is one of the most versatile dishes to have a stash of in your fridge while fasting.

SERVES 4

4 onions
4 garlic cloves
10 peppers, a mixture of red, yellow and orange ones
5 ripe tomatoes
100ml sunflower oil
Sea salt and freshly ground black pepper
A few flat-leaf parsley sprigs, optional

Peel and finely slice the onions and garlic. Halve the peppers, remove and discard the core and seeds, and cut into even sized pieces, around 2–3cm. Score a cross in the top of the tomatoes, place in a heatproof bowl (or pan) and cover with boiling water. Leave for a minute or two, until the skin starts to come away from the flesh, and drain. Peel the tomatoes and then roughly slice or chop the flesh.

Place a wide flameproof casserole on a medium heat, drizzle in the sunflower oil and add all the ingredients. Season generously, with a teaspoon each of salt and pepper, and start to fry. After 10 minutes, reduce the heat to low and fry for around 1½–2 hours. Stir occasionally, until you have a thick, rich and meltingly soft stew. Taste and tweak the seasoning as necessary, then serve, scattered with chopped parsley, if you like.

Braised fennel with saffron

These fennel wedges have it all: sweetness, vibrancy and a perfect punch from the harissa. It's a dish that's a cinch to throw together, and makes a wonderful side, or even a main with a meze of breads, olives and dips.

SERVES 4

- A pinch of saffron threads
- 2 fennel bulbs
- Olive oil
- Sea salt and freshly ground black pepper
- 1 tablespoon honey (or agave, maple syrup or sugar)
- ½ bunch of flat-leaf parsley
- 2 tablespoons harissa paste

Place the saffron threads in 350ml of just-boiled water and set aside to infuse.

Pick any fennel fronds (the little frilly green herb in the middle of the bulb) from the fennel bulbs and keep to one side. Trim the ends and base of the fennel bulbs and cut them into quarters. Lay the wedges out in one layer in a large frying pan and drizzle with a little olive oil, season generously, turn to coat, and place the pan on a medium heat. Fry the fennel for around 10–12 minutes, turning halfway through, until lightly browned all over. Drizzle with the honey and cook for a further 3–4 minutes so the wedges become slightly caramelised. Pour the saffron water into the pan, turn up the heat to bring to the boil, then cover the pan and reduce the heat to low-medium and simmer gently for 15–20 minutes, until the fennel is tender.

Meanwhile, pick and roughly chop the flat-leaf parsley and keep to one side. When the fennel is cooked through, remove the lid and increase the heat to cook away most of the liquid, leaving 5mm at the bottom. Turn the heat off and leave the fennel in the pan to cool slightly. Spoon the harissa onto a serving plate and lay the fennel wedges on top, spoon over a little of the pan juices and sprinkle with the flat-leaf parsley leaves and reserved fennel fronds.

Sweet and sour leeks

I grew up eating leeks cooked this way often – I don't know if it has a particular name, it's just a way of cooking this vegetable that most Greek-Cypriot women seem to know. These leeks are gentle in their contrasting flavours – a little sweetness from the sugar, slow cooking and caramelisation, and the sourness comes from the hit of lemon at the end. This is a delicate side that will happily work with most main meals.

SERVES 4 AS A SIDE

3 leeks
3 garlic cloves
4 tablespoons olive oil
1 tablespoon caster sugar
2 thyme or oregano sprigs, ideally the wild varieties
Sea salt and freshly ground black pepper
1 lemon

Trim the leeks, finely slice the green end and slice the white end into 2cm rounds. Place it all in a colander and rinse thoroughly under cold running water to get rid of any dirt. Peel and finely slice the garlic. Place a large saucepan on a medium-low heat and add the olive oil and sliced garlic. Fry for a minute, then add the sugar and fry for a further 1–2 minutes or until the garlic is lightly golden. Add the washed leeks, pick in the thyme or oregano leaves, and season with a good few pinches of salt and pepper. Fry for about 5 minutes, then add 75ml water, cover with a lid and reduce the heat to low. Cook for 30 minutes or so, stirring from time to time, until softened and sticky. After half an hour, remove the lid, turn the heat up a little and cook for 5 more minutes to get rid of any excess liquid. Squeeze and stir in the juice of the lemon. Taste and tweak the seasoning, then serve.

Above, from top: baklazhannaia ikra (page 122); sweet and sour leeks (opposite)

Baklazhannaia ikra: *poor man's caviar*

Ikra means 'caviar' in Russian – this is a popular way to preserve seasonal vegetables and is eaten throughout Russia and Ukraine. Ikra most commonly has aubergine at the base, but you will find variations with courgettes, or tomato and onion. You don't need a specific reason to make a batch of this – just keep some in the fridge to have as a spread on toast, as a dip, stir through pasta or spoon on top of whatever grains you like. It's a fantastic addition to nearly any meal, but I like it most in a fluffy flatbread with lots of lemon, peppery salad and pickles.

SERVES 6–8

3 aubergines, about 1kg
5 tablespoons sunflower oil
2 red peppers
2 carrots
4 onions
6 garlic cloves
Sea salt and freshly ground black pepper
4 ripe tomatoes
2 tablespoons pepper or sun-dried tomato paste

Preheat the oven to 190°C/fan 170°C/gas mark 5. Pierce the aubergines all over with a fork. Rub with a little sunflower oil and place them in a roasting tray. Pop in the oven for 1 hour, turning them halfway through. When they are soft and cooked through, remove them from the oven and leave to one side to cool slightly.

Meanwhile, halve the peppers, remove the stalk and seeds and finely chop the flesh. Peel and coarsely grate the carrots. Peel and finely slice the onions and garlic cloves. Place a large saucepan on a medium-low heat and add the sunflower oil. Add all of the chopped, grated and sliced vegetables, season well and sauté for 20 minutes, stirring occasionally, until soft and sticky. If it starts to look a bit dry or starts catching, turn the heat right down and cover the pan, stirring occasionally. Finely chop the tomatoes, then stir them into the pan with the pepper or sun-dried tomato paste and continue to cook the vegetables for a further 10 minutes.

When the aubergines are cool enough to handle, cut in half and use a fork to scoop out the filling, shredding it as you go. Shred it directly into a colander in your sink, and press the roasted flesh lightly to get rid of any liquid. Spoon the drained, roasted aubergines into the pan with all the vegetables, and stir everything together. Reduce the heat to low, then cover the pan and cook for 1 hour, stirring often so that it doesn't catch on the bottom. You want the end result to be a rich, thick paste with no liquid in the pan. If it is still a little wet, stir uncovered with the heat turned up a little until it is ready. Taste and adjust the seasoning.

(Photo on previous page)

Skordoxithia koukia: *vinegar-braised broad beans*

I met Greek-Cypriot Margarita Flouri many moons ago, and while I was researching Greek recipes for the book she told me about this treasure. Braising in a vinegar-heavy sauce is something my yiayia had taught me; she often fries whole small fish – such as red mullet – then preserves them in a roux made from flour, garlic, rosemary and vinegar. I've never met anyone else who serves fish this way, so I was fascinated to see another Greek family use the same method, but for a fasting dish. The method for this is so unusual, and the way the recipe cooks down to make a thick dressing for the beans is so surprising and delicious, that if you like broad beans and vinegar (which I do), it may quickly become a favourite.

SERVES 4

2.5kg broad beans (podded weight about 500g – frozen is fine)
2 garlic cloves
3 tablespoons olive oil
2 tablespoons plain flour
1 heaped tablespoon tomato purée
3 tablespoons white or red wine vinegar
Sea salt and freshly ground black pepper
½ bunch of dill or flat-leaf parsley

Pod the broad beans. If they are young, don't worry about double-podding them. However if they are on the larger side, peel off the outer grey skins so you just have the vibrant green beans. Peel and finely chop the garlic. Place a large saucepan on a medium-low heat and add the olive oil and chopped garlic. Fry for a minute or two, until very lightly golden then stir in the plain flour and tomato purée. Fry for a couple of minutes, stirring all the while to make a paste, then stir in the vinegar. Add the broad beans, give them a stir, then add just enough water to cover. Season with sea salt and freshly ground black pepper and bring to the boil. Once boiling, reduce the heat and simmer uncovered for 15–20 minutes, until the beans are cooked and the water has evaporated and thickened to create a perfect dressing. Taste, adjust the seasoning, and leave to cool a little. Finely chop the dill or flat-leaf parsley and stir through. This can be served warm or at room temperature.

Yiahni: *braised peas and other vegetables*

You will find lots of dishes referred to as yiahni in Greek and Cypriot cooking as it's one of the most popular and simple ways to braise vegetables. Yiahni falls under the broad category of *ladera*, in which vegetables are slowly cooked under olive oil (*ladera* means 'oily' in Greek). Traditionally yiahni recipes are very simple, only a few ingredients, and the oil is key for carrying all the flavours. Yiahni are another example of vegetable dishes that really taste better the next day. Serve this with fresh koulouri bread (page 35), pickles such as caper stalks (page 100) or olives and you have a mini meze.

SERVES 4

600g potatoes, Cyprus ideally
80–100ml olive oil
Sea salt and freshly ground black pepper
2 onions
2 garlic cloves
4 carrots
5 ripe tomatoes or 1 x 400g tin of plum tomatoes
1 heaped tablespoon tomato purée
600g baby peas
1 bay leaf
500ml vegetable stock
A few flat-leaf parsley sprigs

Peel the potatoes and cut into large chunks, around 5cm. Pour enough olive oil into a large saucepan or casserole to fill it by 1cm, around 80ml. Place on a medium heat, and fry the potatoes, seasoning as you go, until browned on all sides. Remove from the pan and keep to one side.

Meanwhile, peel and finely slice the onions and garlic. Peel and roughly chop the carrots. If using fresh tomatoes, peel them (see page 287), then roughly chop and keep to one side. After the potatoes are browned, add the onions, garlic and carrots to the same pan, reduce the heat a little and sauté for 10 minutes to soften slightly. Stir in the tomato purée, then after a minute add the chopped or tinned tomatoes, the peas, bay leaf and the vegetable stock. Bring to the boil and let it bubble for 5 minutes, then reduce the heat to low, cover with a lid and simmer for 45 minutes. Check the vegetables: everything should be tender and the liquid thickened. If it still looks a little watery, remove the lid, turn the heat up a little and cook uncovered for 5–10 minutes to reduce down. Remove from the heat and leave for at least 10 minutes before serving. Finely chop the parsley and stir through. Check the seasoning, adding more if need be, and then serve.

Loubye b'zeit: *slow-cooked runner beans with olives*

While flat runner beans are the most traditional type of bean used in this Lebanese dish, you can of course use any type of green bean that is in season and available to you. If you can, make it a day ahead of when you want to eat it – it will be all the more delicious for a bit of time. Serving it at room temperature is totally fine – to be encouraged, in fact. This is lovely as a main meal with fresh bread, crunchy radishes and raw onions, or as part of a meze.

SERVES 4

2 onions
4 garlic cloves
600g runner beans
8 ripe tomatoes
5 tablespoons olive oil
1 tablespoon tomato purée
½ teaspoon ground cinnamon
¼ teaspoon ground allspice
Sea salt and freshly ground black pepper
70g pitted black olives
½ tablespoon red wine vinegar

Peel and finely chop the onions and garlic. Top and tail the runner beans, removing the stringy fibre that runs down the side, then chop into 4cm lengths. Chop the tomatoes into 2cm pieces (ideally peeling them first, see page 287, but if you don't it's not the end of the world).

Pour the olive oil into a large flameproof casserole or big saucepan and place over a medium-low heat. Add the chopped onions and garlic and sauté for 15 minutes, until starting to soften. Stir in the chopped beans, fry for 5 minutes, then add the tomato purée, ground cinnamon and ground allspice. Fry for 1 minute before adding the chopped tomatoes and 300ml of boiling water. Bring to the boil, season generously with salt and pepper and tear in the olives. Once bubbling, reduce the heat to low and cover the pan. Simmer for 30 minutes, until the runner beans are tender. Remove the lid, and turn the heat up to reduce the sauce further if it is still a little watery. Stir in the vinegar, taste and adjust the seasoning. Finish with a good drizzle of extra virgin olive oil and serve once it has cooled a little.

Briam

Not dissimilar to ratatouille, briam is a classic dish that is humble, easy and (given how low-effort it is) astonishingly tasty. You find variations throughout the Balkans, Greece and Turkey: some involve thinly slicing the vegetables and arranging them vertically and neatly in a dish, others are rough and tumble like my method. I love it like this – it maximises the surface area to turn sweet, caramelised and sticky as the vegetables cook. I think this is best served at the table from the dish, with a chunk of fresh bread for mopping up the juices. If you are eating dairy, then a chunk of feta or Cretan mizithra crumbled over the top would not go amiss.

SERVES 8–10

600g Cyprus or other waxy potatoes (you can use small waxy potatoes if that's all you can find)
2 courgettes
4 ripe tomatoes
2 aubergines
2 red onions
2 red peppers
½ bunch of flat-leaf parsley
2 heaped tablespoons tomato purée
1 heaped teaspoon dried oregano
½ teaspoon pul biber, optional
Sea salt and freshly ground black pepper
6 tablespoons olive oil

Preheat the oven to 210°C/fan 190°C/gas mark 6½. If the potatoes are large, you can scrub or peel them if you like – I like to leave the skin on. Cut them into 2cm-thick slices. Slice the courgettes, tomatoes and aubergines into 1cm-thick rounds, discarding the ends, then peel and finely slice the onions. Halve and deseed the peppers and slice into 1cm strips. Pick and chop the parsley leaves and keep to one side, then finely slice the stalks and keep them separate from the leaves. Dissolve the tomato purée in 200ml of just-boiled water.

Place all the sliced vegetables in a large roasting tray. Scatter over the chopped parsley stalks, the dried oregano and the pul biber if using, and season generously with about a teaspoon each of salt and pepper. Drizzle over the olive oil, and massage everything together to evenly distribute the flavours. Spread everything into an even layer and pour over the tomato water. Place in the oven and cook for 1½ hours, checking every 30 minutes to give it all a mix around with a large spoon. The briam is ready when the vegetables are soft but slightly crisp around the edges. If it isn't quite ready, give it another 15–20 minutes. When it's cooked, leave to cool for at least 20 minutes, before finishing with the remaining chopped parsley leaves.

Spiced roasted okra, molasses and herbs

In the past, if you asked me what vegetables I don't like, the only one I could come up with was okra. When it's overcooked, it's slimy. Unfortunately for me, this is the way of most Mediterranean recipes and what I grew up with. When I realised that you can roast or fry it, my opinion changed. Trying it crisp and crunchy, almost like chips, was an okra revelation, and I was all the way on board. I am not averse to frying, but roasting is always easier, and healthier too, so this is now my favourite way of serving these little green spears, sweet and spiced. Just don't tell my yiayia that I think it's better than hers.

SERVES 4

500g okra
½ teaspoon pul biber or dried chilli flakes
¼ teaspoon sweet paprika
1 tablespoon red wine vinegar
3 tablespoons olive oil
Sea salt and freshly ground black pepper
4 spring onions
½ bunch of coriander
½ bunch of mint
1 tbsp pomegranate molasses
2 tablespoons pomegranate seeds

Preheat your oven to 240°C/fan 220°C/gas mark 9. Trim the okra by removing the stalk and snipping off the very tip. Place the spears in a large roasting tray, sprinkle over the pul biber and paprika and drizzle with the red wine vinegar and the olive oil. Season generously and toss everything together well, then spread the okra out evenly. Place the tray in the oven and roast for 20–25 minutes, giving it a shake a couple of times.

While the okra is roasting, trim and finely slice the spring onions. Pick and roughly chop the coriander and mint leaves. When the okra is ready and starting to look crisp, drizzle with the pomegranate molasses as soon as it comes out of the oven. Toss through the sliced spring onion, and serve with the herbs and pomegranate seeds piled on top.

Grilled squash with herbs and dukkah

If you're a fan of squash but not its long cooking time then this is the recipe for you, as cutting it thinly enough dramatically cuts this down. And if you use a grill pan, or a barbecue, you'll get a delicious sweet-charred flavour that is complemented so well with the earthy nuttiness of dukkah. I really do recommend using homemade dukkah, it's a total game changer.

SERVES 4–6

800g butternut squash
3 tablespoons extra virgin olive oil
Sea salt and freshly ground black pepper
½ bunch of flat-leaf parsley
½ bunch of mint
1 lemon
2 tablespoons dukkah (see page 108 for how to make your own)

Place a grill pan on a high heat. Peel and slice the squash into 1cm slices, discarding any seeds. Place in a large bowl and drizzle with two tablespoons of extra virgin olive oil and season generously with salt and pepper. Massage the seasoning into the squash, then grill the slices for 3–4 minutes on each side, until charred in parts and just cooked through. You will have to do this in batches. When the squash is ready, transfer to a platter.

While it is cooking, pick the herb leaves into a mixing bowl and finely grate over the lemon zest. Squeeze over the lemon juice, stir in the remaining olive oil, season a little and toss together. When all the squash is cooked, toss through the herb mixture and sprinkle with the dukkah.

Maroulla's spiced courgettes

Almost collapsing courgettes, with little joyous bits of caramelised onion and sticky sweet garlic dotted throughout... This could be one of my favourite sides, and it is most definitely my favourite way to cook courgettes. There aren't very many ingredients, so it's important to really take care over each step in the simple method, starting with the way the courgette is cut. Whenever courgettes were in season, my yiayia Maroulla would cook them like this, slowly so they became soft and creamy, then (if she wasn't fasting) ripple in beaten eggs at the last minute. She would serve them alongside every meal, and you could usually find a little bowl of leftover, room-temperature courgettes on the kitchen worktop. They will always remind me of her.

SERVES 4 AS A SIDE

3 garlic cloves
1 onion
500g courgettes
3 tablespoons olive oil
Sea salt and freshly ground black pepper
½ teaspoon Lebanese seven-spice (see page 111 for how to make your own)
¼ teaspoon pul biber or dried chilli flakes

Peel and finely slice the garlic cloves and onion. Trim the courgettes then cut into 2–3cm thick slices or chunks. My favourite way is to cut them in small wedges: so slice off the top straight, then slice the next piece of courgette at 45-degree angle, next slice straight, next at an angle. Pour the olive oil into a wide frying or saucepan on a medium-low heat and add the garlic. Place on a medium-low heat and fry for a few minutes, until the garlic is lightly golden. Add the sliced onion and courgettes to the pan and season generously with salt and pepper. Turn the heat up to medium and fry for a couple of minutes, then cover the pan with a lid. Cook for 10 minutes, covered, stirring halfway through. Then remove the lid, stir in the spices, reduce the heat lightly and fry for a further 10–15 minutes so that any liquid cooks away, and the vegetables are soft, sticky and golden around the edges. The courgettes should almost be falling apart and very soft. Taste and adjust the seasoning, then serve.

(Photo on page 88–89)

Arnabeet: *deep-fried cauliflower with tarator*

My mum makes a classic Cypriot dish called *kounoupidi yiahni*, cauliflower florets that are deep-fried then braised with sweet tomatoes. It's utterly delicious, and the fried cauliflower element is irresistible – we usually snaffle so much as it cooks that I'm surprised any makes it into the end dish. So when I first read about Lebanese arnabeet I knew it was going to be my kind of dish. The tarator sauce is a little like the tashi on page 94, but thinner, just a drizzle to cut through the fried cauliflower. And if the idea of deep frying puts you off, you can roast the cauliflower: season the florets, toss with a few tablespoons of olive oil, arrange on a tray in a single layer and roast at 240°C/fan 220°C/gas mark 9 for 20–25 minutes, until golden-brown and crisp.

SERVES 4–6

1 large head of cauliflower (around 1kg with leaves)
1 litre vegetable oil
¼ teaspoon sweet smoked paprika
Sea salt and freshly ground black pepper
1 teaspoon sumac
½ bunch of flat-leaf parsley
1 lemon

Tarator dressing

1 garlic clove
Sea salt and freshly ground black pepper
3 tablespoons tahini
1 lemon

Cut the cauliflower into equal-sized florets and wash well with cold water. Spread out on a tea towel and leave to dry completely. Meanwhile, make the tarator dressing. Peel and roughly chop the garlic clove and place in a pestle and mortar. Pound till creamy with a good pinch of salt and pepper then muddle in the tahini and the juice of the lemon. Add two tablespoons of cold water and mix together, adding more if it is too thick – you're looking for something about the consistency of double cream or slightly thicker. Taste and adjust the seasoning, then set aside until ready to serve.

When you are ready to fry the cauliflower, pour the oil into a large saucepan and place on a medium heat. Line a large plate with kitchen paper. Place the cauliflower pieces in a large bowl, sprinkle over the paprika and season generously with a few good pinches of salt and pepper. Toss the cauliflower until all the florets are coated. Place a small piece of cauliflower into the oil and when it starts to sizzle and turn golden brown, the oil is ready. If you have a thermometer, the oil should be about 170°C, then when you add the cauliflower it will drop to about 160°C. Fry the seasoned cauliflower florets in batches, so as to not overcrowd the pan, for 4–5 minutes, until crisp and golden all over. Transfer them to the paper-lined plate. When all the florets are cooked, pile them up on a platter or serving plate, sprinkle with sumac and drizzle over the tarator sauce. Roughly chop the parsley and scatter it over. Cut the lemon into wedges, and serve on the side, for squeezing over.

(Photo on page 89)

Eleni's artichoke tava

Tava is one of my all–time Cypriot favourites: the tender lamb, sweet tomatoes, fragrant cumin, and potatoes and/or rice, all seemingly thrown together at random but creating a cohesive whole, makes it a true one-dish wonder. So when fellow Greek-Cypriot Maria Repanos told me her mum, Eleni, made a fasting version with artichokes, I knew immediately I had to give it a try – and once I had, I knew I had to ask her permission to print it here. I've tweaked the method slightly, for ease, but other than that it is all Eleni's recipe. And I am eternally grateful to her for sharing it with us.

SERVES 6

2 lemons
6–8 violet or small globe artichokes
4 carrots
3 large onions
5 ripe tomatoes
100ml sunflower or olive oil
2 tablespoons tomato purée
1 tablespoon ground cumin
1 teaspoon ground cinnamon
200g medium or long grain rice
Sea salt and freshly ground black pepper
A few flat-leaf parsley sprigs

Halve one of the lemons and squeeze all of the juice into a large bowl of water – you'll need this to prepare the artichokes. Using a serrated knife, trim off the top of the artichokes and a good chunk of the stem. Peel or cut away the tough outer leaves, leaving the tender inner leaves. Trim down the stem to remove the tough skin. Then halve the artichokes and use a teaspoon to scoop out the choke (the fuzzy bit in the middle). Cut the artichokes into 2cm-thick slices, and rub them with the cut lemon halves to stop them browning, then place them in the water.

Peel the carrots and slice into 2cm-thick rounds. Peel and slice the onions into 2cm-thick wedges. Score the tops of the tomatoes with a cross and submerge into a bowl of just-boiled water. Leave to one side for 5 minutes, then drain and peel off the skin. Roughly chop the flesh.

Preheat your oven to 190°C/fan 170°C/gas mark 5. Place a wide flameproof casserole dish (that has a lid) on a medium heat and pour in the oil. Fry the drained sliced artichokes for 8–10 minutes, until lightly golden, then add the onions and carrots and turn the heat down a little. Fry for 5 minutes then stir in the tomato purée and chopped tomatoes. Fry for a couple of minutes, then stir in the cumin and cinnamon, and then stir in the rice. Season generously and keep stirring until all the rice is coated with the oil and flavourings and well mixed in with the vegetables. Meanwhile, boil a kettle then pour in 700ml of boiling water, so that the rice is just covered, and cover the dish. Place in the oven and cook for 25 minutes, so that everything is perfectly cooked. Remove the lid, turn the oven temperature up to 220°C/fan 200°C/gas mark 7 and cook for a further 10 minutes until gold and crisp on top. Leave to rest for 5 minutes. Roughly chop the parsley, and serve scattered over the tava, with the remaining lemon cut in wedges on the side.

Crushed coriander and olive potatoes

This recipe isn't a traditional *nistisimo* recipe as such, but Lent happens in spring here, when the new potatoes come in, so I really associate eating these potatoes with fasting times. Greek-Cypriots love lemony roast spuds with crushed coriander seeds, and the black olives add such fun, intense bursts of flavour, making this such a great side to have with any roast.

SERVES 4 AS A SIDE

750g new potatoes
2 teaspoons coriander seeds
Olive oil
½ lemon
Sea salt and freshly ground black pepper
60g pitted black olives, such as kalamata
½ bunch of coriander, optional

Preheat the oven to 220°C/fan 200°C/gas mark 7. Bring a large pan of salted water to the boil. Place the potatoes in the pan and boil for 15 minutes, or until almost cooked through. Drain and leave them to steam dry in the hot pan. Transfer to a roasting tray and carefully crush the potatoes, either with the heel of your hand or with the back of spoon or a fish slice. Crush the coriander seeds using a pestle and mortar (these don't have to be too fine) and sprinkle over the potatoes with a few tablespoons of olive oil, the juice of the lemon and a good amount of seasoning. Tear in the olives, toss to combine, then roast for 20–25 minutes, until golden and crisp. When the potatoes are ready, roughly chop the coriander leaves, if you like, then scatter and serve.

Batata harra: *chilli-dressed potatoes*

In Arabic, *batata harra* simply means 'spicy potatoes', and you'll find many variations of this much-loved dish across the Middle East. Usually, the potatoes are deep fried, or boiled then fried. For ease, I roast mine, but the method of cooking the spuds is up to you – the key element here is how you dress them: I like some sweet smoky paprika in with my chilli flakes.

SERVES 4

800g large waxy potatoes, Cyprus or red-skinned ideally
Olive oil
Sea salt and freshly ground black pepper
1 onion
3 garlic cloves
1 bunch of coriander
1 teaspoon pul biber or dried chilli flakes
¼ teaspoon sweet smoked paprika
¼ teaspoon turmeric
½ lemon

Preheat your oven to 210°C/fan 190°C/gas mark 6½. Traditionally, the potatoes would be peeled, but I like leaving the skin on, so it's up to you. Cut the potatoes in 3cm cubes and place in a roasting tray big enough to hold them in one layer, then drizzle with a couple of tablespoons of olive oil. Season, toss together well, and place in the oven for 50 minutes, or until golden all over and cooked through.

While the potatoes are cooking, make the dressing. Peel and finely chop the onion and garlic. Pick the coriander leaves, finely chop the stalks and roughly chop the leaves. Place a small frying pan on a medium-low heat and drizzle in three tablespoons of olive oil. Add the chopped onion and garlic and sauté for 15 minutes until starting to soften (if it starts to catch, add a splash of water). Stir in the pul biber, sweet smoked paprika, turmeric, the finely chopped coriander stalks and half the coriander leaves, and fry for a further minute then remove from the heat. When the potatoes are ready, stir through the cooked garlic mixture and the remaining chopped coriander. Squeeze over the juice from the lemon and serve immediately.

Taro two ways

If you are lucky enough to live near an international greengrocer, you may have seen taro but not known what it is or what to do with it. Popular throughout south Asia, the Middle East and Africa, taro is a starchy root vegetable that is bulbous, brown and often a bit muddy-looking on the outside. However, the flesh when cooked becomes tender and almost buttery. The main tip for cooking taro is that it must be cracked into chunks and not cut. If you cut it straight with a knife, you will end up with a slimy finish, a bit like the texture of slow-cooked okra. Also, it does need to be boiled properly, as it contains harmful toxins (these can also be removed by soaking the cut chunks overnight in cold water but if it is boiled well it is fine).

Kolokassi: *tomato and celery braised taro*

In Cyprus, we slow-cook taro with tomato, carrot and celery. It is called kolokassi and is one of my favourite winter foods, providing our diet with much needed warmth and sweetness during the short, darker days. It often includes chunks of pork or chicken, then as Easter approaches and Lent kicks in the meat is left out. To be honest, I rarely miss it as this is a hearty dish as it is.

SERVES 6

1.8kg taro
6 tablespoons olive oil
Sea salt and freshly ground black pepper
4 onions
6 celery sticks
6 carrots
4 flat-leaf parsley sprigs
2 heaped tablespoons tomato purée
1 × 400g tin of plum tomatoes
1 lemon

Peel the taro. Now, you don't want to cut it, you want to break the flesh. Insert a sharp knife no more than halfway into the taro, then carefully put pressure on it and twist a little so that the taro cracks. Repeat this with the taro pieces, so you create smaller pieces – you are looking for 4–5cm chunks. Place the olive oil in a large saucepan or flameproof casserole over a medium heat. Fry the taro chunks for about 15 minutes, seasoning them as they fry and turning so they are golden all over (you will probably have to do this in batches).

While the taro is frying, prepare the rest of the vegetables. Peel and chop the onions. Trim and cut the celery in 1–1.5cm slices. Roughly chop any little pale leaves from the inside the celery, if you have the heart. Peel and slice the carrots to a similar thickness. When the taro has all been fried, place in a bowl and reduce the heat under the pan a little. Add all the chopped vegetables and whole parsley sprigs to the pan and sauté for 15 minutes. When they are looking sticky, stir in the tomato purée and fry for a couple more minutes. Add the tomatoes to the pan and break them up with a wooden spoon. Add enough water to the pan to just cover all the vegetables, squeeze in the juice from the lemon, season well and stir. Bring to the boil, then cover the pan, reduce the heat to low, and cook for 45–60 minutes. The taro needs to be tender but you don't want the pieces to be falling apart. When it is ready, remove the lid, turn the heat up and reduce the sauce a little. Taste and tweak the seasoning as needed, then leave to cool a little before serving.

Oulas: *taro soup with coriander, dill and lemon*

The Egyptian way of cooking taro, called oulas (or sometimes kolkas), is wetter than the recipe I have grown up with, more like a chunky soup than a stew. It is fresher and brighter, laced with paste made from chard, coriander and garlic. My school friend Amirah Sami introduced me to oulas, and tells me it has a huge significance in the Coptic Christian diet. Egyptian Copts celebrate Epiphany on 19th January, as their year is based on the ancient Egyptian calendar, and the majority of Coptic Christians will celebrate by feasting on oulas. There are parallels between taro and Christ's baptism, including the boiling of the taro (which helps eliminate toxins in the root), reminding us of being purified of sin when we are dunked into baptismal water. As the skin of the taro is removed before being eaten, so are we removed of our robes of sin when we are baptised; and the green paste from the chard and herbs symbolises new life. There is even an Arabic children's rhyme which says that 'if you don't eat oulas, you'll wake up with no head' – *rass* is the word for head in Arabic. No wonder everyone makes sure to eat it!

I haven't blitzed my greens for my version of oulas, as I love the chunky chard pieces. However, if you want to be more authentic, then feel free to purée the garlic and greens first, then fry the paste until dark and add this to the broth.

SERVES 4

750g taro
1.2 litres vegetable stock
6 garlic cloves
400g Swiss chard
1 bunch of coriander
½ bunch of dill
5 tablespoons olive oil
1 heaped teaspoon ground coriander
Sea salt and freshly ground black pepper
1 lemon

Peel the taro and break it, don't cut it. Insert a sharp knife no more than halfway into the taro, then carefully put pressure on it and twist a little so that the taro cracks. Repeat until you have 2–3cm chunks.

When you are ready to cook, place the stock in a large saucepan over a high heat and bring to the boil.

Peel and finely chop the garlic. Trim and finely slice the chard. Trim the herbs and finely chop them, stalks and all. Place another large saucepan or frying pan on a medium-low heat and add the olive oil and garlic. Sauté for 2 minutes until lightly golden, then add the ground coriander, and then all the sliced chard and half of the chopped herbs. Season generously with salt and pepper, then fry for 25 minutes, until the greens have cooked down and darkened.

When the greens are ready, rinse the taro and place into the boiling stock. Cook for about 15 minutes over a medium heat, or until tender, then stir in the cooked greens. Add the remaining chopped herbs and squeeze in the juice of the lemon. Taste, adjust the seasoning, and serve.

Shchi: *cabbage and caraway soup*

This hearty soup is a staple of Russian cuisine. There are lots of variations depending on region and season: green shchi made with sorrel or nettles; a sour version made with sauerkraut; some with meat. This fast-friendly version is incredibly comforting, simple and needs no adornment apart from a slice of rye bread. However, if you are eating dairy, you could add a dollop of sour cream to your bowl.

SERVES 4–6

2 onions
4 garlic cloves
1 leek
2 carrots
400g waxy potatoes
500g white cabbage
4 tablespoons sunflower oil
2 tablespoons tomato purée
1 teaspoon caraway seeds
¼ teaspoon sweet smoked paprika
1.5 litres vegetable stock
2 bay leaves
Sea salt and freshly ground black pepper
½ bunch of dill

To serve: Rye bread

Peel and finely chop the onions and garlic. Trim and finely slice the leek, then rinse it well in a colander to get rid of any dirt. Peel the carrots and potatoes, the chop them into 2cm pieces, keeping them separate. Halve the cabbage, remove the core, and finely shred the leaves. Place the sunflower oil in a large casserole or saucepan over a medium-low heat. Add the onions, garlic, leek and carrots and sauté for 15 minutes, until softened and sticky. Stir in the tomato purée, caraway seeds and paprika, then after a minute add the shredded cabbage, chopped potato, vegetable stock and bay leaves. Turn up the heat and bring to the boil. Season generously, then reduce the heat to a simmer. Cook on a low heat for 1 hour, until the vegetables are tender and the broth is rich. Taste and tweak the seasoning. Leave for 10 minutes before serving. Finely chop the dill, then ladle the soup into bowls and serve scattered with dill, and a slice of rye bread on the side.

Pepper-braised cabbage wedges

This recipe, based on *varză calita* – a classic Romanian cabbage dish – is one to convert any cabbage avoiders. It is sweet and tender, the perfect side to any large meal. The addition of toasted walnuts came about after a conversation with Romanian food writer Irina Georgescu. She told me of another cabbage dish, *varză dulce*, mostly eaten during times of fasting due to the absence of oil (walnut oil is the occasional exception in Romania, due to the trees being in abundance in the Subcarpathian mountains). It is made by simmering cabbage and tomatoes until soft, and finished with walnuts to for fat and flavour. If you are strictly fasting, then feel free to remove the sunflower oil from this recipe, and start by griddling the cabbage. Simmer the onions and pepper in water, with the lid on to soften, and go from there.

SERVES 4

1 white cabbage, around 900g
5 tablespoons sunflower oil
Sea salt and freshly ground black pepper
3 onions
1 red pepper
2 tablespoons tomato purée
½ teaspoon sweet paprika
1 × 400g tin of plum tomatoes
1 tablespoon caster sugar
1 bay leaf
300ml hot vegetable stock
1 lemon
50g walnuts, optional

Trim the cabbage, removing any tatty outer leaves, and cut into eight wedges. Cut out a little of the thick core, but leaving a little in place to hold the leaves together (having said that if they fall apart it isn't the end of the world – just makes them harder to fry). Place a wide flameproof casserole or large frying pan on a medium heat and add three tablespoons of sunflower oil. Season and fry the cut sides of the cabbage wedges for around 8–10 minutes, turning halfway through, until charred – this will give it amazing flavour overall. While the cabbage is searing, peel and finely slice the onions. Halve the pepper, remove the seeds, and finely slice. When the cabbage is ready, keep to one side, turn the heat down a little and sauté the sliced onions and pepper for 10 minutes, adding the remaining 2 tablespoons of sunflower oil and seasoning them well. When they are soft, add the tomato purée and sweet paprika to the pan, fry for a couple of minutes then add the plum tomatoes, sugar, bay leaf and stock. Bring to the boil, breaking the tomatoes up with your wooden spoon, and season well. Once the sauce is boiling, gently nestle in the cabbage wedges, cut side up, and squeeze over the juice of half of the lemon. Season, cover the pan with a lid and reduce the heat to low. Cook for 45 minutes, until the cabbage is tender.

Meanwhile, if using the walnuts, preheat your oven to 180°C/fan 160°C/gas mark 4. Place the walnuts in a small ovenproof dish and toast in the oven for 8 minutes. Leave to cool then roughly chop. When the cabbage is ready, remove the lid from the pan, stir in the chopped walnuts and turn the heat up. Cook for a further 10–12 minutes, so that the sauce has reduced and is thickened. Taste, adjust the seasoning and squeeze in lemon juice to taste.

Erene's nistisimo keftedes

My neighbour and friend Erene Panteli runs our local Greek-Cypriot deli with her mum and sister (the shop's details are on page 291). She is the main chef there and everything she makes tastes like home. Other than making the dishes vegan during times of fasting, she doesn't attempt to tamper with them, they're pure Greek-Cypriot nostalgia and I love that. Everyone does – customers travel far and wide for her food. One of her two most popular dishes is her keftedes (Greek-Cypriot deep-fried meatballs) which are perfect – just like my maternal yiayia's. The other is her vegan keftedes, which are outstanding, as good as – and very like – the meat ones. I've tried lots of vegan and vegetarian keftedes and these are by far the best. They're lovely piping hot with houmous (page 90) or tashi (page 94) but equally I do love them cold, straight from the fridge the next day.

MAKES ABOUT 35

4 baking potatoes, around 700g
2 carrots
1 onion
1 courgette
2 plum tomatoes
½ bunch of flat-leaf parsley
200g dried breadcrumbs
½ × 400g tin of chopped tomatoes
1 tablespoon fine sea salt
1 tablespoon dried mint
½ tablespoon ground black pepper
1–1.5 litres vegetable oil, for frying
Flaky sea salt, to finish

Using a box grater or a food processor, grate the potatoes and carrots through the small holes. Peel the onion, then grate it, the courgette and tomatoes using the coarse side of the grater, or a larger food processor attachment. Finely chop the parsley, stalks and leaves. As each vegetable is grated, place into your largest mixing bowl, then add all the remaining ingredients, except the oil. Using your hands, mix everything together until evenly combined. Set the bowl aside for 15 minutes.

Get some trays ready: you'll need a couple for the uncooked keftedes and a couple that are lined with kitchen paper, ready for the cooked ones. Place the oil in a large deep pan – you want it to be at least 6cm deep – and place on a high heat. While it is heating, shape the keftedes. Take a small amount, about a heaped tablespoon, in your hand, squeeze it a little to discard any extra moisture and shape into balls, or use the natural curve of your palm to shape into rounded oblongs. Shape all the mixture, placing the keftedes on the trays as you go.

When the oil is hot, about 170°C, carefully place the keftedes in the oil, about six at a time, depending on the size of your pan. Once they have a bit of colour, you can give them a gentle stir or prod, in case they need help releasing from the bottom of the pan – don't do it too soon or they will fall apart. When they are a nice brown colour, after about 4 minutes, remove from the pan to the kitchen paper-lined trays to absorb the oil, and sprinkle with flaky salt. Repeat with the remaining mixture, then serve and eat.

Manitaria stifado: *wild mushrooms, onions and garlic in wine*

Stifado is, of course, one of the defining dishes of Greek cuisine – a boldly flavoured and aromatic stew of beef and whole onions. For Greek-Cypriots, our family includes a surprising number of non-meat eaters, so mushroom stifado is something my yiayia makes regularly, not only during times of fasting. This is such a warming, hearty dish and so rich with savoury flavours that I promise you no one will mind the absence of meat. Serve with bulgur wheat, pilaf or fluffy rice.

SERVES 4

600g very small or baby onions
1kg wild mushrooms
4 garlic cloves
4 tablespoons olive oil
1 teaspoon ground allspice
Sea salt and freshly ground black pepper
4 thyme sprigs
3 bay leaves
1 cinnamon stick
200ml red wine
200ml tomato passata
2 tablespoons red wine vinegar

Bring a large pan of water to the boil. Remove from the heat and add the unpeeled onions to the pan. Leave for 2 minutes, then remove. This will make them easier to peel, which you want to do carefully, leaving them whole if possible. Trim and wipe the mushrooms clean, tearing any large ones in half. Peel and finely slice the garlic.

Preheat your oven to 200°C/fan 180°C/gas mark 6. Place a large flameproof casserole on a medium-low heat and add the olive oil and peeled onions. Fry for 5 minutes then add the sliced garlic and allspice. Fry slowly for another 5 minutes, just so that everything is lightly golden. Add the wild mushrooms to the pan, season well, pick in the thyme leaves and fry for 5–10 more minutes – until the mushrooms have released their moisture and start to become golden. Don't stir them too often, allow them to get some colour from the pan. Add the bay leaves, cinnamon stick and red wine to the pan and turn up the heat. Bring to the boil and let it all bubble for a couple of minutes to reduce the wine a little. Add the passata and red wine vinegar and bring to the boil again, and then cover the casserole with a lid. Transfer to the oven and cook for 35 minutes, removing the lid for the last 15 minutes, until the onions are soft and the sauce is rich and reduced.

Alissa's borscht

Even if you aren't hugely clued-up on Eastern European cuisine, the chances are you have heard of borscht. As food writer Alissa Timoshkina explains in her book *Salt and Time*: 'Borscht to Eastern Europe and Russia is like houmous to the Middle East. We all eat it, we all love it, yet we simply can't imagine that any other country owns the rights to it.' And as much as Alissa loves a good traditional borscht, she admits to sometimes struggling with eating a 'plateful of chunky discoloured vegetables that have given all their best to the broth'. This is her solution. I particularly love how the broth develops over time – if you can make it the day before you will be rewarded with a deeper flavour.

SERVES 4

6 garlic cloves
1 onion
1 carrot
Sunflower oil
6 red beetroots
2 red peppers
2 tablespoons tomato purée
Sea salt and freshly ground black pepper
2 bay leaves
1 tablespoon black peppercorns
1 tablespoon coriander seeds
1 tablespoon fennel seeds
1 bunch of dill
½ bunch of flat-leaf parsley
500g sauerkraut
2 tablespoons pomegranate molasses
1 red onion
1 tablespoon brown sugar
1 × 400g tin of kidney beans
2 teaspoons sweet smoked paprika

To serve: Dairy-free sour cream, optional

Peel the garlic. Peel and finely chop the onion. Peel and grate the carrot. Pour a tablespoon of sunflower oil into a large saucepan and fry the onion and carrot over a medium heat for 8 minutes, until softened and the onion is golden. While that's happening, peel and grate two of the beetroots. Halve one of the peppers, remove the seeds and finely slice the flesh. Add that all to the pan with the onions, then stir in the tomato purée and a splash of water. Season well, and fry for a further 5–8 minutes. When it has all started to soften, pour over 2 litres of water and add the bay leaves, peppercorns, coriander seeds, fennel seeds, four of the peeled garlic cloves and half of the dill and half of the flat-leaf parsley. Season with a tablespoon of salt and bring to the boil. Reduce the heat, finely grate in the remaining two garlic cloves and add half the sauerkraut with its brine and simmer, covered, over a low heat for 1 hour. Turn off the heat and let the borscht rest for another hour or so, while you prepare the rest of the elements.

Here is where the recipe starts to deviate from tradition quite a lot: to prepare the vegetables that will grace the plate and also add extra flavour and texture to the soup, you will need to do a bit of roasting. Preheat your oven to 180°C/fan 160°C/gas mark 4. Peel the remaining four beetroot, then cut them into wedges and place in a roasting tray. Drizzle with sunflower oil, season with salt and the pomegranate molasses. Peel the red onion, cut into thin wedges and season with salt and the brown sugar to bring out its sweetness. Place in the roasting tray with the beetroot and roast together for 30 minutes. Drain the kidney beans, then dress them with salt, oil and the smoked paprika. Core and deseed the remaining pepper, then cut into thin strips and dress with salt and oil. Roast the beans and pepper together in a roasting tray, as they will need only 10–15 minutes.

When all the vegetables are ready, strain the broth through a fine sieve or a muslin cloth, discarding the solids. Reheat the broth. Next create layers of texture and flavour in each bowl by adding a heaped tablespoon of the remaining sauerkraut to each, as well as a handful of roasted beetroot, onion, kidney beans and red pepper. Top each bowl with the hot broth. Chop the remaining dill and flat-leaf parsley, and sprinkle over the top. Serve with a spoon of dairy-free sour cream, or regular, if you prefer.

Prassinopita: *celebration of greens pie*

If you're wondering about the authenticity of this recipe... I made it up. *Prassino* means 'green' in Greek, and as all our pies end in *pita*, I smushed the words together because a green pie is exactly what this is.

I've said it before and I'll keep saying it: salting is the most effective way to prepare greens (crucially spinach) for pies. Wilting them never gives the same level of flavour. It takes a bit of time, but it's more than worth the minimal effort.

SERVES 6

400g strong white bread flour, plus a little extra
2 teaspoons fine sea salt
1 tablespoon caster sugar
½ × 7g sachet of fast-action dried yeast
Olive oil
1 medium courgette, around 200g
1 leek
4 spring onions
200g baby leaf spinach
¼ teaspoon fennel seeds
1 bunch of dill
½ bunch of flat-leaf parsley
1 teaspoon freshly ground white pepper
1 lemon
2 tablespoons sesame seeds
3 tablespoons honey (or agave syrup)

Place the strong white bread flour in a large mixing bowl (or the bowl of a free standing mixer) and whisk in one teaspoon of the fine sea salt. In a jug mix together the caster sugar and yeast with 225ml of warm water. Leave for a few minutes. Use your fingers to rub in four tablespoons of olive oil to the flour (or use a dough hook), then make a well in the middle. Mix in the yeast water, adding a few more tablespoons of water if the dough needs it to come together – you don't want it to be dry. Turn out the dough on a lightly floured surface, and knead for 8–10 minutes, until smooth and elastic. Alternatively use a free-standing mixer with a dough hook to do this for you. Transfer the kneaded dough to a clean, lightly oiled bowl and leave to prove for 1 hour.

While the dough is proving, prepare the filling. Trim and slice the courgette lengthways, the finely slice each half. Trim and slice the leek in the same way, then place the finely sliced leek in a colander and rinse thoroughly to remove any grit. Trim and finely slice the spring onions. Place them all in a large colander with the baby leaf spinach and scrunch in the remaining teaspoon of fine salt, really turning the vegetables. Leave the colander in the sink for 30 minutes, scrunching it all together again halfway through.

Preheat your oven to 220°C/fan 200°C/gas mark 7. Grind the fennel seeds using a pestle and mortar. Finely chop the dill and flat-leaf parsley. Scrunch the filling in the colander one last time and really squeeze out the excess liquid – it should look as if the greens have been wilted down and cooked slightly. Transfer to a large mixing bowl. Add the chopped dill and parsley, the white pepper and the juice from the lemon, and mix through the greens with your hand.

Turn the dough out to a lightly floured work surface and pat into a ball. Roll or push the dough out into a circle, about 35cm diameter, and heap the salted greens in the middle of the dough. Bring the sides up over the filling and join them together in the middle so you have a big pie. Drizzle a little oil into a 24cm ovenproof frying pan and carefully transfer the pie to the pan, patting and easing it in, seam-side down, so it fills the pan. Drizzle the top of the pie with a little more olive oil and pat on the sesame seeds and ground fennel seeds. Place the pan on a medium heat and fry for 2–3 minutes, or until it starts to sizzle, then transfer the pan to the oven. Bake for 25–30 minutes, or until golden all over. Remove the pie from the oven and drizzle with the honey. Leave to stand for 5 minutes before serving warm – it's also really nice at room temperature.

(Photo overleaf)

Opposite: prassinopita (page 156)

Mushroom, potato and cumin bourekia

Little pies with similar names but varied fillings feature across the eastern Mediterranean, Eastern Europe and Middle East. This recipe uses a ready-made puff pastry, which incidentally happens to be dairy free, so they're vegan and simple to make. And the filling is packed with flavour, so they're delicious to grab for a quick snack or to have with a salad in a larger meal.

MAKES 20

500g chestnut mushrooms
1 onion
2 garlic cloves
1 waxy potato, about 200g
4 thyme sprigs
5 tablespoons olive oil, plus extra for the trays
Sea salt flakes and freshly ground black pepper
½ teaspoon ground cumin
2 × 320g sheets of dairy-free puff pastry

Trim and wipe clean the mushrooms, then chop into 1cm pieces. Peel and finely chop the onion and garlic cloves. Peel and coarsely grate the potato. Pick the thyme leaves. Place a large frying pan over a medium heat and add three tablespoons of olive oil. Add the mushrooms, onion, garlic and thyme leaves. Season well with half a teaspoon of sea salt and quarter of a teaspoon of freshly ground black pepper, and fry for 15 minutes. Halfway through, stir in the grated potato and ground cumin. The filling is ready when the mushrooms have released their moisture and started to turn golden, and the potato is just tender. Turn off the heat and leave the filling to cool.

When you are ready to make the bourekia, preheat your oven to 220°C/fan 200°C/gas mark 7. Grease two baking trays with a little oil. Have a small bowl of cold water to hand. Unroll the puff pastry sheets and cut out 20 circles that are 9cm in diameter. You may need to cut and smooth together the edges of some of the trimmings to get the last couple of circles on each sheet. Spoon a heaped dessertspoon of the mushroom mixture into the centre of each circle of pastry. Dip your finger in the cold water and run around the edge of the pastry and fold half over to enclose the filling, creating a semi-circle shape. Pinch the edge of the pastry together, then use a fork to press the join firmly together. Place the pies on the greased baking trays and brush the tops of each with a little oil and sprinkle with a pinch of flaky sea salt. Bake for 18–22 minutes, or until golden and risen. Leave the pies to cool for at least 5 minutes on the tray before eating them.

Kolokithopita: *pumpkin and raisin pie with harissa*

This one of my go-to *nistisimo* recipes if I have people round for a meal – you can get it ready in advance, it looks impressive and it tastes amazing. It is loosely based on the Greek-Cypriot fasting classic *kolokotes* – little pumpkin, bulgur and raisin pies – that my yiayia Martha makes. Roasting the pumpkin first is not traditional, my yiayia just uses finely chopped raw pumpkin, but I think it brings a more intense flavour to the dish, which I balance with harissa oil and dill.

SERVES 4

800g pumpkin or butternut squash
125ml olive oil
1 teaspoon sea salt
Freshly ground black pepper
1 teaspoon ground cinnamon
1½ tablespoons harissa paste
1 tablespoon caster sugar
40g fine bulgur wheat
50g sultanas or raisins
4 spring onions
½ bunch of dill
300g filo pastry
1 garlic clove

Preheat the oven to 240°C/fan 220°C/gas mark 9. Peel and chop the pumpkin into 2cm pieces and place in a roasting tray with three tablespoons of the olive oil, half a teaspoon of sea salt, a good pinch of freshly ground black pepper, the ground cinnamon, one tablespoon of the harissa paste and the sugar. Toss together well, spread out into one even layer and pop in the oven for 25–30 minutes, until the pumpkin is charred around the edges. Remove from the oven, spoon into a bowl and leave to cool. When the pumpkin has cooled, stir in the bulgur wheat and sultanas or raisins. Trim and finely chop the spring onions and dill. Add all the spring onions and half of the dill to the bowl and mix everything together, crushing and mashing the pumpkin pieces down a bit.

When ready to bake, preheat your oven to 220°C/fan 200°C/gas mark 7. Brush a 22cm springform cake tin with a little oil. Lay out a sheet of filo, longest side nearest to you, and brush with oil, then top with another sheet. Spoon one-third of the mixture in a line about 4cm above the bottom edge of the pastry, then brush the pastry with more oil. Roll the pastry and filling up like a cigar then curl it into a swirl; this is the centre of your pie. Place the filled swirl in the middle of the cake tin. Repeat the filling and rolling process with the remaining sheets of filo and filling, adding each length to the pie spiral, so you have a coiled snake effect. Brush the entire pie with a little more oil and sprinkle with the remaining salt. Bake for 35–45 minutes, until crisp and deep golden brown.

While the pie is baking, make the finishing oil. Crush the garlic, in its skin, with the side of your knife and place in a small pan with four tablespoons of olive oil. Gently fry over a low heat, until it starts smelling wonderful but it doesn't burn – about 4 minutes. Remove the pan from the heat and immediately stir in the remaining half-tablespoon of harissa. Leave to cool. When the pie is ready, brush with the harissa garlic oil, discarding the garlic clove, and leave the pie to stand for at least 15 minutes. Serve sprinkled with the remaining chopped dill.

Father Augustine's kebbet laktin

Father Augustine is a Lebanese monk who lives in a monastery in Dbayeh, north-east of Beirut. They grow and cook a lot of fresh produce, including the pumpkins used for this, one of his favourite fasting meals. You may already be familiar with fried kibbeh (or koupes as we call them in Cyprus), little grenades of spiced mince in a crisp bulgur shell. This vegan version is baked in a tray, so it's less fiddly. Inspired by reading Claudia Roden's *Arabesque*, I've tweaked Father Augustine's recipe to make it open-topped, so the 'shell' is more like the bottom crust of a tart, which makes it easier to put together, and lighter to eat.

SERVES 6–8

1kg pumpkin or butternut squash, or 400g pumpkin purée
1 onion
250g fine bulgur wheat
½ teaspoon ground cinnamon
¼ teaspoon ground allspice
Sea salt and freshly ground black pepper
3 tablespoons plain flour
100ml olive oil
5 red onions
2 garlic cloves
200g baby leaf spinach
1 teaspoon cumin seeds
½ teaspoon pul biber or dried chilli flakes
3 tablespoons pomegranate molasses
2 tablespoons toasted pine nuts

If you are using fresh pumpkin, peel and deseed the pumpkin, then chop the flesh into 3cm chunks. Place the pumpkin in a large pan, cover with water and bring to the boil over a high heat. Reduce to a simmer and cook until the flesh is tender, 20–30 minutes. Drain in a colander and leave to steam dry for 30 minutes so that all the excess liquid evaporates. Peel and finely chop the onion and set aside.

Once the pumpkin is cooled and dry, you should have around 400g. Transfer to a large mixing bowl and blitz to a purée with a stick blender. Stir in the chopped onion, fine bulgur wheat, cinnamon and allspice, and season with a quarter-teaspoon each of salt and pepper. Leave the mixture to one side for 30 minutes, so the bulgur wheat has a chance to absorb the moisture from the pumpkin. Stir in the plain flour till combined, then use your hands to knead the mixture until you have a smooth dough. If the mixture is looking dry and crumbly, very gradually add enough water to bring it together – depending on the pumpkin you may need to add up to six tablespoons. This is OK, just keep going slowly until it all comes together.

Preheat your oven to 220°C/fan 200°C/gas mark 7. Brush a deep, loose-bottomed 24cm fluted pie tin with a little oil (I find larger flutes work better with this recipe). Press the pumpkin-bulgur dough evenly into the base and up the sides of the tin. Drizzle generously with olive oil, and gently brush it round so that everything is covered; brush up the fluted edge, or tilt the tin, so that the outer crust has a slick of oil too. Place the tin in the oven and bake for about 35 minutes, until the crust is golden all over and the top of the edge is slightly browned.

While the crust is cooking, make the filling. Peel and finely slice the red onions and garlic. Rinse the spinach well, and set aside to drain. Place a wide pan on a medium-low heat and add three tablespoons of the olive oil. Add the sliced onions and garlic and cook for 10 minutes, covered, until they have started to soften. Stir in the cumin seeds, pul biber and a teaspoon each of sea salt and freshly ground black pepper. Fry for a further 15 minutes, with the lid off, stirring occasionally, until sticky and sweet. Stir in the pomegranate molasses and cook for a further 5 minutes – the onions should be gloriously pink. Add the spinach, turn up the heat a little and cook for 8–10 minutes, until all the leaves have wilted and there is hardly any moisture left in the pan. When both the filling and crust are ready, spoon the filling into the case. Remove from the tin and slide onto a serving board. Finish by sprinkling over the pine nuts and leave to stand for 5 minutes before serving.

(Photo overleaf)

Father Augustine's kebbet laktin (page 164)

4 — *Pantry – pulses and grains*

If vegetables are the stars of the show when it comes to eating *nistisimo*, larder staples like pulses and grains are the backbone to a meal. Growing up we would often refer to recipes using these ingredients as 'peasant food' – inexpensive meals for when there is little else. With just a few simple ingredients and a bit of time, you can make a hearty, wholesome dinner. Eating in this way still remains my favourite. Recipes made with little fuss – like beans, cooked slowly with vegetables and finished with a little *kalo lathi* (good olive oil) – may be rustic food but they can confidently take a place on the finest table.

Revithosoup: *houmous soup*

Houmous soup may sound like some modern social-media-style mash-up recipe, but it is a very traditional Greek recipe. Father Andreas Christodoulou, my uncle, taught me how to make *tahinosoupa*, a recipe that the priests often eat while fasting that is (as it sounds) a soup thickened with tahini – vegan but creamy and flavourful. Houmous soup takes this to another level – it's richer, with more of a punch due to the garlic and paprika. You can of course cook your own chickpeas, which would undoubtedly make the soup more delicious, but using jarred (or tinned) chickpeas is so easy it then becomes a regular weeknight feature.

SERVES 4–6

2 onions
1 carrot
2 celery sticks
4 tablespoons olive oil, plus extra to serve
500g cooked chickpeas (see page 289) or jarred/tinned chickpeas (drained weight, liquid reserved)
1 garlic clove
4 tablespoons tahini
Sea salt and freshly ground black pepper
1–2 lemons
A few flat-leaf parsley sprigs
Sweet smoked paprika, to taste
2 tablespoons toasted sesame seeds

Peel and chop the onions and carrot. Trim and chop the celery. Place a large saucepan on a medium-low heat and add the olive oil and chopped vegetables. Sauté for 15 minutes, until the vegetables are starting to soften and become sticky and sweet, then add the chickpeas and 500ml of cooking water (or any liquid from the jar or tin, if using). Bring to the boil, then reduce the heat to a simmer and cook for 20 minutes.

When the soup mixture has cooked for 20 minutes, peel and roughly chop the garlic clove and add to the pan along with the tahini and generous pinch of salt and pepper. Blitz with a stick blender, until smooth and creamy. Squeeze in the juice of one lemon, stir and taste. Tweak the seasoning by adding more lemon, salt and pepper to taste. Depending on what chickpeas you used (and if you used any chickpea liquid) you may need to add an additional 100–250ml of just-boiled water to reach a consistency you like. Pick and finely chop the parsley leaves. Serve the soup in bowls, finished with a drizzle of olive oil and the chopped parsley scattered, plus a sprinkle of paprika and toasted sesame seeds.

Roasted squash, lentil and coriander soup

The inspiration for this soup is *shorbat adas*, a staple of Arabic cuisines and often eaten to break fasts during Ramadan. I like to make soups like this for my family during Lent, and other times of fasting, and bulk them out with seasonal vegetables such as squash or pumpkin. Usually, I drizzle the vegetables with oil and roast them to bring out their sweetness. However, I once made some for Father John Hookway, the priest at our local Greek Orthodox church, on the day before Orthodox Easter Sunday – a day he doesn't eat oil. Instead, I simply boiled all the ingredients together in the stock, and blitzed it till smooth. He loved it, so play around with the method depending on why and when you are making it.

SERVES 4–6

- 1 small butternut squash, around 750g
- 2 red onions
- 3 tablespoons olive oil
- 1 teaspoon ground coriander
- ½ teaspoon ground cumin
- Sea salt and freshly ground black pepper
- 2 litres vegetable stock
- 1 teaspoon ground turmeric
- 75g red lentils
- ½ lemon
- A few coriander sprigs

Preheat your oven to 210°C/fan 190°C/gas mark 6½. Trim and peel the butternut squash. Cut in half, remove the seeds, then cut into 3cm chunks. Peel the onions and cut into large wedges. Place the vegetables in a large roasting tray, drizzle over the olive oil, then sprinkle with the ground coriander, ground cumin and a good pinch of salt and pepper, and toss to combine. Place in the oven and roast for around 45 minutes, or until the squash is cooked through and caramelised around the edges.

Meanwhile, pour three-quarters of the stock into a large saucepan and add the turmeric and lentils. Bring to the boil over a high heat, then reduce to a simmer and cook for 25 minutes. When the squash and onions are ready, scrape them into the saucepan with the lentils and simmer for a further 5 minutes. Blitz the soup with a stick blender until mostly smooth – a bit of texture is nice. Add the extra stock, if you prefer it thinner, and bring the soup back to a simmer. Just before you are ready to eat, squeeze in the juice from the lemon half, then taste and tweak the seasoning. Roughly chop the coriander and sprinkle over the top before serving.

Kibbet el raheb: *monks' soup*

As fascinating as it is delicious, some people say Jesus, and some say Mary, ate kibbet el raheb. Whether that's true or not, this ancient Lebanese soup is traditionally only eaten on Good Friday – for some Christians, it is the only thing they eat that day. However, I think it really is too good to not be enjoyed year round, being both therapeutic to make and restorative to eat. The little dumplings that go in the soup have a similar texture to kibbeh and are particularly moreish. To be honest, there are always a few less in the soup than there should be when I make it.

SERVES 4

1 shallot or small onion
100g plain flour
75g fine bulgur wheat
½ teaspoon ground allspice
½ teaspoon ground cinnamon
Sea salt and freshly ground black pepper
6 mint sprigs
½ bunch of flat-leaf parsley
Olive or vegetable oil
2 garlic cloves
2 red onions
250g spinach or Swiss chard
150g brown lentils
2 tablespoons pomegranate molasses
½ lemon

Peel and chop the shallot as finely as you can and place in a bowl with the flour, bulgur wheat, allspice, cinnamon and a quarter-teaspoon each of salt and pepper. Pick the mint and parsley leaves and finely chop them together, then add half to the bowl and set the rest aside. Add 6 tablespoons of cold water, then use your hands to bring the mixture all together until you have a firm dough. Knead in the bowl for 5 minutes until the dough is consistently smooth then roll into 2cm balls and lay out on a tray. You should get about 45 little dumplings.

Place a large saucepan on a medium-low heat and add four tablespoons of oil. Fry the dumplings for around 12–15 minutes, turning, until lightly browned all over. You will probably need to do this in batches. Spoon the browned dumplings back on to the tray and keep to one side.

Peel the garlic and red onions and finely slice. Add them both to the pan with a little more oil and fry for 15 minutes or so, until golden brown. Wash the spinach or chard, trim the ends and roughly slice the leaves and finely slice the stems, then add it all to the pan with the lentils and pomegranate molasses. Stir for a minute then cover with 1.5 litres of cold water and turn up the heat. Bring to the boil, then cover, reduce the heat and simmer for 30 minutes. Add the dumplings back to the pan and cook for a further 20 minutes. Just before you want to serve, squeeze in the lemon juice, stir in the remaining chopped herbs and adjust the seasoning to taste.

Rishta: *lentil and pasta soup*

Big claim time: this Lebanese soup is my favourite recipe in this chapter, and one of my favourites in the whole book. Having grown up on a diet filled with lentils, I adore them, and the addition of chopped-up pasta makes this soup rich and thick, as the starch gives it a velvety texture. Cumin, coriander, garlic and lemon are the holy quartet of flavours in my world, and the best bit is that this is pretty effortless to throw together. Also, it tastes great the next day. If you try only one recipe in this book, make it this one.

SERVES 4–6

200g green lentils
1.8 litres hot vegetable stock
2 onions
4 garlic cloves
4 tablespoons olive oil
1 bunch of coriander
1 teaspoon cumin seeds
1 teaspoon ground coriander
125g tagliatelle
Sea salt and freshly ground black pepper
½ lemon

Rinse the lentils thoroughly under running water, and pick out any stones. Place in a large pan with the hot stock and bring to the boil. Reduce the heat to low and simmer for 45 minutes. Meanwhile, peel and finely slice the onions and garlic. Place a large frying pan over a medium-low heat and add the olive oil and sliced vegetables. Sauté for 15 minutes, until softened and just coloured. Finely chop the coriander. Stir the cumin seeds and ground coriander in with the onion and fry for a minute. Stir in half the fresh coriander to the frying pan, fry for a further 2 minutes, then remove from the heat.

When the lentils are ready, stir in the sautéed onion mixture. Roughly break the tagliatelle into smaller pieces and add to the soup. Season generously with salt and pepper and bring back to the boil. Reduce the heat and simmer for a further 5 minutes, or until the tagliatelle is just cooked. Squeeze in the juice of the lemon half and finish with the remaining chopped coriander before serving.

Fava, pickled onions and capers

There are two recipes in here that are actually from my previous book, *Taverna* – this and my houmous recipe on page 57 – but to not include them in a book about fasting food would be unthinkable. Fava in particular, as it is a dish that is often eaten on *Kathara Deftera* (Clean Monday) along with lagana bread (page 29). Apologies if you have both books, but hopefully you agree and understand. On the days that seafood is allowed, fava is traditionally served with pickled octopus. (If you are vegan, obviously disregard this next bit.) I recommend tracking down a jar of octopus, or even squid, to serve alongside it. If you really want to push the boat out, buying an uncooked octopus and simmering it for an hour with aromatics, and then barbecuing it, would be even better.

SERVES 6

300g dried yellow split peas
2 onions
2 garlic cloves
5 tablespoons extra virgin olive oil
4 rosemary sprigs
Sea salt and freshly ground black pepper
1 bay leaf
1 red onion
2 lemons
2 tablespoons capers

Place the yellow split peas in a sieve and rinse under running water. Peel and finely chop the onions and garlic. Place a large saucepan on a medium-low heat, pour in three tablespoons of olive oil and add the chopped vegetables to the pan. Pick in the rosemary leaves, season, and gently sauté the onion mixture for 10 minutes until soft and sticky but not coloured. Stir in the washed split peas and the bay leaf and pour in 1 litre of boiling water. Turn the heat up, bring it all to the boil then reduce the heat to low and cover with a lid. Cook gently for about 40 minutes, until the water has all been absorbed and the fava is thick and creamy. Periodically check during cooking and spoon off any white scum that comes to the surface, topping up with more boiling water if needed – don't let it cook dry as it needs to be creamy.

While the fava is cooking, peel and finely slice the red onion. Squeeze over the juice of half a lemon, and leave to one side to soften.

When the fava is ready, discard the bay leaf, season generously and use a stick blender to blitz to a smooth purée. Squeeze in the juice from the remaining 1½ lemons and pour in a couple of tablespoons of extra virgin olive oil. Check the seasoning and beat it all together. Serve the creamy fava topped with dressed sliced onions and the capers.

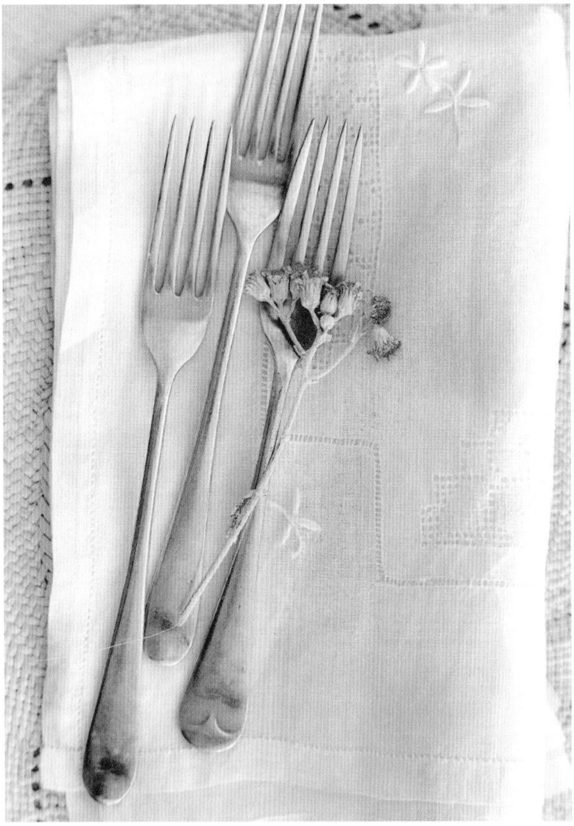

Black-eyed beans, chard and lemon

Black-eyed beans, what Greek-Cypriots call *louvi*, are often referred to as peasant food because they're a true Cypriot pantry staple, eaten throughout the year with whatever vegetables are in season. In the summer, the beans are cooked still fresh, in their pods with sweet, yellow-fleshed marrow (*kolokoui*), while in the colder months the dried beans are eaten with chard. This dish is so simple, yet embodies everything I adore about Greek Orthodox fasting food: it's comforting, fresh, simple and inexpensive.

SERVES 4

250g dried black-eyed beans, or 2 × 400g jars/tins of beans
2 onions
2 garlic cloves
1 leek
200g Swiss chard
75ml olive oil
Sea salt and freshly ground black pepper
2 lemons
½ bunch of flat-leaf parsley
A few dill sprigs

Wash the dried black-eyed beans and remove any that don't look good. Place in a large pan of cold water and bring to the boil. Cook for 50–60 minutes, or until just tender.

While the beans are cooking, peel and finely slice the onions and garlic. Trim, wash and finely slice the leek. Trim and slice the chard stalks, and roughly chop the leaves. Place a second large pan on a medium heat and add the olive oil. Fry the sliced onion, garlic, leeks and chard stalks for 15 minutes, until starting to soften, then add the chard leaves and cook for a further 5 minutes. When the black-eyed beans are ready, or if you're using jarred or tinned beans, strain and add to the pan with the vegetables. Cover with just enough fresh water to cover and season well. Bring to the boil, then reduce the heat a little and simmer for 15 minutes with the lid on, then remove the lid and turn the heat up and cook for a further 5 minutes to reduce the liquid. The beans should be tender and there should be just enough liquid to loosen them, but it shouldn't be soupy. Squeeze in the juice of one lemon to taste, then taste before adding any more. Finely chop the herbs and stir them in, then taste to check the seasoning before serving.

Prebranac: *caramelised-onion baked beans*

A classic of Serbian cuisine, and popular during times of fasting, this simple dish is far greater than the sum of its parts: beans and a few aromatics. Make it and you'll find yourself eating it in various forms over the course of a few days – as with most bean dishes, it gets better over time. Eat as is or with the peppers on page 116, or any of the salad or vegetable recipes, to be honest.

SERVES 8

500g dried butter beans, or 4 × 400g jars/tins of butter beans, drained and liquid reserved
1 bay leaf
6 onions
8 garlic cloves
100ml sunflower or olive oil
1 tablespoon sweet paprika
Sea salt and freshly ground black pepper
A few flat-leaf parsley sprigs, optional

To serve: Crusty bread

If you are cooking the beans from scratch, first soak the dried beans for about 12 hours in plenty of cold water. After that time, drain the beans and place them in a large saucepan with the bay leaf. Cover with three times as much water and place the pan on a high heat. Bring to the boil, then reduce the heat and simmer for about 1½ hours, or until the beans are tender. Do not let them boil dry. Drain the cooked beans, reserving the cooking liquid.

Preheat the oven to 200°C/fan 180°C/gas mark 6. While the beans are cooking, peel and finely slice the onions and garlic. Place the oil in a large flameproof casserole or ovenproof pan and add the sliced onions. Sauté the onions slowly over a medium-low heat for about 30 minutes, until golden and sticky. If the onions start to catch even a little, add a splash of water. Add the sliced garlic and paprika for the final 10 minutes.
Stir in the drained beans, 750ml of the cooking liquid (or liquid from the jars/tins) and season generously. If you need to, make up the amount of liquid with just-boiled water from a kettle. Place the uncovered casserole in the oven and cook for around 1–1½ hours. Check the beans a couple of times during cooking and add a splash more cooking liquid (or water from the kettle) if the dish looks like it is drying out. The end result should be golden on top, with soft and oozy beans underneath. Remove the casserole from the oven and set aside to let the beans cool, to serve warm or at room temperature. Finish by roughly chopping the parsley, if using, and scattering over the top, then serve with crusty bread.
The beans are even better reheated the next day, or day after.

Lobio: *spiced kidney beans, walnuts and coriander*

I was talking to food writer Olia Hercules about fasting and Lenten foods in Ukraine and she showed me pamphlets published by Orthodox priests about foods to be eaten during fasting times. I have never seen anything like this in Greek churches, but I loved them – everyone needs a little encouragement and inspiration on a diet, regardless of what it is for. The pamphlets featured lots of Georgian and Central Asian recipes (as Olia pointed out, an echo of the Soviet Union), which makes sense: many Georgian dishes are rich in nuts, so ideal for sustaining people for long periods of time. Lobio came up time and again. Variations of this dish (*lobio* translates to 'beans') can be found throughout Georgia – not all have walnuts, and the herbs and spices will vary, but I wanted to feature one that seemed popular with the priests.

You can of course make this with tinned beans, which is still fine and makes it a much speedier recipe. However, as with all these recipes, it really is more delicious if you cook the beans yourself. By adding the cooking liquor back into the dish, it makes it richer, creamier and more flavourful. Never throw that liquid away, it is your secret ingredient.

SERVES 4–6

400g dried kidney beans or
3 × 400g jars/tins of beans
2 bay leaves
3 onions
120g walnuts
1 large bunch of coriander
4 garlic cloves
½ teaspoon dill seeds, optional
¼ teaspoon cayenne pepper
1 teaspoon ground coriander
Sea salt and freshly ground
black pepper
1 pomegranate
4 tablespoons olive oil
3 tablespoons pomegranate molasses
Extra virgin olive oil

Soak the dried kidney beans overnight in plenty of cold water. When you are ready to cook them, drain, and place in a large saucepan with the bay leaves and cover with plenty of fresh cold water. Bring to the boil then simmer for 1–1½ hours, until the beans are very tender.

Meanwhile, peel the onions. Finely chop two and a half of them, and finely slice the remaining onion half. Finely chop or grind the walnuts. Trim the coriander stalks and finely chop the stalks and leaves. Peel the garlic. Place the garlic in a mortar with the dill seeds (if using), cayenne pepper and ground coriander and quarter of a teaspoon each of salt and pepper. Grind until you have a creamy texture, then add two-thirds of the chopped coriander and pound that in too. Halve the pomegranate and carefully pick the seeds, and keep to one side.

Pour the olive oil into a large saucepan and sauté the chopped onions for 15 minutes over a medium-low heat, until cooked through and slightly golden. When the beans are ready, drain in a colander (reserving a large mugful of the cooking liquid) and return them to the warm pan. If you are using jarred or tinned beans, start with this step. Season generously, then use a wooden spoon, or even a potato masher to crush them so they break down. Spoon them into the pot with the onions and add the chopped walnuts, the garlicky spice paste, one tablespoon of the pomegranate molasses and half the reserved cooking water. Mix and crush everything together well until creamy, and return the pan to the heat and cook for 5 minutes. Add the remaining cooking liquid if needed, so that the beans aren't too dry, and taste to adjust the seasoning as necessary. Spoon the seasoned beans into a serving bowl. Finish by drizzling over the remaining pomegranate molasses and a good amount of extra virgin olive oil, then garnish with the reserved coriander, pomegranate seeds and onion slices.

Fasoles: *slow-cooked beans and garden vegetables*

Fasoles can be a hard recipe to sell; as a bean stew, it can be just fine or it can be incredible. If you've ever been to Greece or Cyprus you will know that the simple, often tomatoey, soft beans are always one of the best dishes in a taverna. There are three key steps to elevating this from fine to incredible: sauté the base vegetables until they are sweet; cook the beans low and slow; and, most importantly, do not be shy with the olive oil. It is crucial to the flavour of the dish, as is finishing it with a slick of extra virgin olive oil. I'm not here to lecture you on good and bad fats, but olive oil is often cited as a factor in the Mediterranean lifestyle being one of the healthiest in the world. Plus, if you are adopting a plant-based diet, short or long term, then it is essential that it is well balanced, and that includes fats.

SERVES 8

- 500g dried white beans (white kidney, cannellini, haricot), or 4 × 400g jars/tins of beans
- 2 onions
- 4 carrots
- 4 celery sticks
- 1 leek
- 400g waxy potatoes, Cyprus ideally
- 100ml olive oil
- 2 heaped tablespoons tomato purée
- 5 flat-leaf parsley sprigs, plus extra, optional, for serving
- 2 bay leaves
- Sea salt and finely ground black pepper
- Extra virgin olive oil – to finish (this is important, please don't leave this out)

Start the night before by soaking the dried beans in plenty of cold water.

The next day, peel and crudely chop the onions and carrots. Trim and slice the celery sticks and leek into pieces 1–1.5cm thick. The vegetables are to be celebrated, not just a base, so you don't want to chop them finely. Rinse the leek slices thoroughly in a colander to get rid of any dirt. Peel the potatoes and cut into 3cm chunks. Place a large flameproof casserole or saucepan over medium-low heat and add the olive oil. Add the chopped onion, carrot, celery and leek to the pan and sauté for 20 minutes, stirring occasionally, until they're losing moisture and turning sweet and starting to soften. Stir in the potatoes and tomato purée and fry for a couple of minutes. Boil a full kettle of water. Add the drained dried or tinned beans to the other vegetables. Pour in enough boiling water to cover everything by 2cm. Add the parsley sprigs, bay leaves and season generously with salt and pepper – around a teaspoon of each – and bring back to a boil. Cover the pan, reduce the heat to low and simmer for 2½ hours, until the beans are tender. Remove the lid, and if the beans are looking liquidy, turn the heat up and bubble away for about 15 minutes, so that the fasoles become creamy and the liquid reduces and thickens. Taste and add more seasoning as required. Ideally leave the beans to sit for a few hours before serving, or even better overnight, as they become more delicious with time. Serve with a drizzle of extra virgin olive oil and a gesture of chopped parsley, if you like.

Maghmour: *aubergine and chickpea stew*

This Lebanese recipe is often called moussaka, which may confuse you if you only know the Greek dish of the same name, yet there are various versions of moussaka throughout Eastern Europe and the Middle East. If you look at the ingredients you can see how it changes as it travels. In Lebanon it is the recipe below – an aubergine and tomato base, with chickpeas as the protein. In Turkey it has a similar stew-like form, but meat replaces the chickpeas. This then becomes the familiar Greek version, with the components layered and topped with a white sauce. And by the time you get to the Balkans, it is almost identical to the Greek version, but with potato in the layers rather than aubergine.

I have never found a Greek-style moussaka that I liked in vegan form, so when I am fasting and want that kind of aubergine recipe, I often make maghmour or even briam (page 129): both are familiar, comforting *nistisimo* dinners.

SERVES 4

2 large or 3 medium aubergines
3 onions
6 garlic cloves
100ml olive oil
Sea salt and freshly ground black pepper
1 heaped tablespoon tomato purée
½ teaspoon cayenne pepper or dried chilli flakes
1 × 400g tin of plum tomatoes
400g cooked, peeled chickpeas (see page 289) or 2 × 400g jars/tins of chickpeas, drained
½ tablespoon dried mint

Trim the aubergines, and use a speed peeler to remove most of the skin, leaving a 'striped' effect, and then cut into 4cm chunks. Peel and chop the onions. Peel and finely chop the garlic. Line a plate with kitchen paper. Place a large flameproof casserole on a medium heat and add the olive oil. Fry the aubergine in batches, for 5 minutes each side, so that they become golden. Season generously with sea salt and black pepper while cooking. Spoon onto the paper-lined plate, and repeat until all the aubergine is fried. Add the chopped onion and garlic to the pan, reduce the heat a little and sauté for 15 minutes, until softened and caramelising. Then, stir in the tomato purée and cayenne pepper, fry for a minute then add the tinned tomatoes and break them up with a wooden spoon. Add 400ml of water and bring to the boil. Add the cooked, jarred or tinned chickpeas to the pan with the aubergine, then sprinkle over the dried mint and reduce the heat a little. Simmer for 30 minutes, until everything is combined, soft and thickened. Turn off the heat and leave to stand for at least 10 minutes before serving.

Ta'ameya: *broad bean falafel*

While falafel are commonly thought of as a chickpea-based snack, classic Egyptian falafel, called ta'ameya, is made with fava (dried broad beans). This is eaten throughout the year, but even more so during times of fasting, and it is often claimed to be more delicious than the classic chickpea version. To judge, you'll simply have to make this recipe...

You can't make these with tinned or jarred fava beans as these beans will be cooked, and you need the fava to be raw to keep their shape.

SERVES 4
(MAKES ABOUT 25 FALAFEL)

300g dried split fava beans
1 red onion
2 garlic cloves
1 bunch of flat-leaf parsley
½ bunch of coriander
1 heaped teaspoon ground coriander
1 teaspoon ground cumin
¾ teaspoon fine sea salt
1 teaspoon bicarbonate of soda
30g toasted sesame seeds
1 litre vegetable oil
Flaky sea salt
2 lemons

To serve: All the trimmings – pita bread, tomato, sliced onions, tahini dressing or houmous, pickled chillies... and whatever else you like with falafel

Start this recipe the night (or morning) before by soaking the fava beans in plenty of cold water. Let them soak for at least 8 hours.

To make the ta'ameya, peel and roughly chop the onion and garlic. Trim and roughly chop the flat-leaf parsley and coriander. Place them all in a mixing bowl along with the ground coriander, ground cumin and sea salt. Drain the fava beans in a colander, and gently dry with kitchen paper. Stir them through the chopped herb and veg mixture until well mixed in then spoon into the bowl of a food processor. Pulse until roughly chopped then add the bicarbonate of soda and continue to pulse until you get a consistent dough. You don't want a fine paste, which is why it is important to pulse and not leave the motor running, otherwise it will be too fine. Line a large tray with greaseproof paper and use a tablespoon measure to scoop heaped balls of the mixture and place on the tray – they should be around the size of a ping pong ball. Sprinkle them with the toasted sesame seeds and lightly pat them down so they have evenly flattened surfaces on the top and bottom.

When ready to fry the ta'ameya, heat the oil in a large saucepan over a medium heat. While it heats, cut the lemons in wedges and get the pita, salad and other accompaniments ready. Line a large plate or shallow bowl with kitchen paper. Test the oil is ready by putting a small cube of potato or bread in it. When it is golden, the oil is hot enough; if you have a thermometer, you're looking for the oil to be 165–175°C. Fry the patties in batches for 3–4 minutes, then flip over and fry for a further 1–2 minutes, until browned all over. Use tongs or a slotted spoon to transfer the ta'ameya to the kitchen paper to absorb the excess oil, and sprinkle with flaky sea salt. Serve straight away with all the trimmings, and wedges of lemon to squeeze over.

Azadouhi's vospov kofte: *spiced red lentil balls*

While I was researching recipes for this book, a woman called Sharice Babakhani gave me invaluable insight into the fasting food of the Armenian diaspora, told through the experiences of her grandmother Azadouhi. Azad, as she is known in her family, was born in Adana, Turkey, the first child of her parents to be born after her father escaped the Armenian genocide of the first world war. Her name means 'freedom' in Armenian.

When Azadouhi was a small child, the family moved to Cyprus, where they lived in Omorphita, and she attended the well-known Armenian Melkonian school in Nicosia. There is a huge Armenian community in Cyprus, however during the 1974 war that divided the country, many Armenian families once again had to find new homes. Azadouhi and her family moved to the Greek territory of Cyprus, then to the UK in search of a better future.

Azadouhi lived to be 100 years old, and throughout her life had an open-door philosophy, feeding her family and guests for all the big celebrations, and fasting according to Orthodox traditions. This recipe of hers was totally new to me, but is now very much part of my repertoire. You can also find another of Azadouhi's recipes on page 254: anoush abour, which has a beautiful and ancient religious story.

SERVES 6–8

3 onions
2 bunches of flat-leaf parsley
3 tablespoons olive oil, plus extra, optional, for the salad
200g red split lentils
200g fine bulgur wheat
1 teaspoon ground cumin
Sea salt and freshly ground black pepper
3 ripe tomatoes
½ teaspoon sumac
1 lemon, optional

Peel and finely chop the onions. Finely chop the flat-leaf parsley, stalks and all. Place a large saucepan on a medium-low heat and add the olive oil and one-third of the chopped onions. Fry for 15 minutes, or until golden and soft. Stir in the red split lentils and cover with 1.25 litres of water. Turn up the heat, bring to the boil, then reduce to a simmer and cook for 25 minutes, or until the lentils are very soft. Drain the lentils and onion in a sieve over a bowl, so that you remove most of the excess water but reserve it for when you start kneading. The vegetables don't need to be bone dry, but they shouldn't be sopping wet. Transfer the lentils and onions to a large mixing bowl, then stir in the fine bulgur wheat, half the remaining chopped onion, one-third of the chopped parsley, the ground cumin and a half-teaspoon each of sea salt and freshly ground black pepper. Mix together then knead with your hands to form a paste – add as much of the drained water as you need to get a smooth mixture; it shouldn't be dry, and you may need to add all of the reserved liquid, and even a touch more from the tap. Keep kneading, then take a small ball of the mixture and form with your hands into a small, two-bite kofte. Leave the indents of your fingers on the mixture.

Halve the tomatoes and scoop out the seeds and flesh. Finely chop the flesh and mix in a small bowl with the remaining chopped onion and parsley. Add the sumac, season well and stir to combine.

To eat, take a kofte and press it into the salad to make it stick, mopping up some of the juices as you go, and eat together. Or, less fun, you can dress the salad with the juice of the lemon and a little olive oil, and place on a plate with the kofte, to eat with a fork.

Jewelled moutzentra

Various forms of this lentil dish, which you likely know as mujadara, are popular throughout the Middle East; some with tomato, others with just onion, spiced or with herbs. You can think of it as a rice side, but we often eat this Cypriot version as a main meal with a vinegary chopped salad, and thick Greek yoghurt if we're not fasting.

SERVES 4–6

Sea salt and freshly ground black pepper
250g dried green or brown lentils
130g long grain rice
4 onions
3 garlic cloves
4 tablespoons olive or sunflower oil
1 teaspoon cumin seeds
½ pomegranate
1 bunch of flat-leaf parsley
50g toasted flaked almonds
50g dried sour cherries
½ lemon

Place a large pan of salted water on to boil. Thoroughly rinse the lentils in a sieve, picking out any stones, and then cook in the boiling water for 20 minutes, until almost cooked. Meanwhile, rinse the rice in a sieve, then add to the pan for a further 12 minutes, until perfectly cooked – the rice isn't meant to be mushy (although if I am making it just for me, I do like it a little mushy and so add an extra 2 minutes). Drain the rice and lentils in a sieve or fine colander, and return to the hot pan to steam dry and keep fluffy.

While the lentils are cooking, peel and finely slice the onions and garlic. Place a large frying pan on a medium heat and pour in the oil. Sauté the onions, garlic, cumin and a good pinch of salt and pepper for 20 minutes, until deep golden brown. To encourage them, I cover the frying pan with a lid for 10 minutes, adding a splash of water if needed, then fry uncovered for 10 minutes. Stir occasionally. While that's happening, pick the pomegranate seeds. Pick and roughly chop the flat-leaf parsley leaves, and toss them with the toasted flaked almonds, sour cherries and pomegranate seeds. Squeeze over the juice from the lemon half, and toss it all together. When the onions are ready, stir through the cooked lentils, check the seasoning and plate up. Garnish with the dressed fruits and nuts and serve.

Mushroom and caramelised onion pilaf

There are countless versions of this kind of rice dish throughout the Mediterranean, Middle East and Eastern Europe – think pilau, pilafi, plov, paella and beyond! In fact, cooking grains (usually rice, sometimes wheat) in stock or water with spices, herbs, and often vegetables and meat, is a technique found across the world. This mushroom and sweet onion pilaf is one of my family's favourites, robust enough to be eaten as a main meal.

SERVES 4

- 2 onions
- 2 garlic cloves
- 500g mixed mushrooms
- 4 tablespoons olive oil
- 15g dried wild mushrooms
- 50g vermicelli pasta
- 200g long grain rice
- Sea salt and freshly ground black pepper
- 1 bunch of dill
- 1 lemon
- 40g toasted pine nuts
- A few pinches of pul biber, optional

Peel and finely slice the onions and garlic. Wipe, trim and roughly slice the mushrooms. Place a large flameproof casserole or saucepan on a medium-low heat and drizzle in half of the olive oil. Stir in the onions and garlic and sauté for 15 minutes, stirring occasionally, until softened and a little coloured. While that's happening, place the dried mushrooms in a measuring jug, cover with boiling water and leave to one side. When the onions are soft and golden, stir in the sliced fresh mushrooms. Break in the vermicelli pasta, so that you have small pieces around 2–3cm long, then stir in with the mushrooms and onions, and turn the heat up. Fry for 5 minutes, until everything takes on a little more colour. Meanwhile, remove the dried mushrooms from their soaking water, reserving it for later. Slice the dried mushrooms add them to the pan, then also add the rice and stir everything together well and season generously. Top the reserved mushroom soaking liquor with enough boiling water to bring it up to 800ml and pour into the pan with the rice mixture. Bring to the boil, then reduce the heat to very low and cover. Cook for 20–25 minutes, stirring only once or twice. Finely chop the dill and keep to one side.

The pilaf is ready when all the water has been absorbed. Remove the pan from the heat, and squeeze in the juice of the lemon. Stir in the dill, then taste and adjust the seasoning. Spoon on to a platter and finish with sprinklings of toasted pine nuts and pul biber, if using.

Gemista: *roasted stuffed vegetables*

In Greek homes, stuffed vegetables are just as popular as the more well-known dolmades (stuffed vine leaves, page 204). If you find the idea of making dolmades or dolma intimidating then gemista are a good place to start; you don't have the bother of hunting down vine leaves, because you can stuff whatever seasonal vegetables are available to you. As well as the vegetables below, you can also use aubergines or blanched white cabbage leaves. It's a longer recipe than many in this book, but it is relatively simple and incredibly rewarding to make. Just zone out and think of it as meditative dish that also doubles as a crowd pleaser – it's perfect for when you're having people round as you don't want to serve them piping hot, so they can be made ahead with little stress.

SERVES 6–8

4 onions
8 tomatoes
2 round courgettes, if you can get them, or red peppers
75ml olive oil
Sea salt and freshly ground black pepper
2 tablespoons tomato purée
250g medium grain rice (you can use a mixture of short and long grain, however paella rice is probably most similar to the Greek rice traditionally used)
2 teaspoons dried mint
1 teaspoon ground cinnamon
½ bunch of flat-leaf parsley
650ml hot vegetable stock
1 lemon

To get ahead, I prepare the onions the night before – they need time to cool down before you stuff them. Cut off the top and bottom and peel off the skin. Make a vertical slice in the onions, halfway into the centre, so that once they are boiled you can peel off the layers in one piece. Place the onions in a large saucepan and cover them with water. Bring to the boil over a medium heat and cook for 40 minutes, till tender throughout. Remove the onions from the water and leave to cool completely.

When you are ready to cook the gemista, slice the tops off the tomatoes and the courgettes (or peppers). Set the tops aside to use later, and scoop out the middle of the vegetables – be careful to not scoop out too much of the tomatoes or they will fall apart. Put the tomato filling in a bowl to one side, but discard the seeds from the courgettes or peppers. Arrange the prepped vegetable shells in a roasting tray, leaving space for the stuffed rolled onions too.

Separate the onion layers, carefully easing them off one by one – you probably only want the first four or five layers from each onion. Finely chop the central onion core. Pour three tablespoons of the olive oil in a wide saucepan over a medium-low heat and fry the chopped onions for 10 minutes. Add half a teaspoon each of sea salt and freshly ground black pepper to the fried onion, then stir in one tablespoon of tomato purée. After a minute, roughly chop the reserved tomato flesh and add it to the pan, then continue to cook until most of the juices have reduced and you are left with a just little liquid in the bottom of the pan (this will be soaked up by the rice). Stir in the rice, dried mint, ground cinnamon and season with salt and pepper. Finely chop the parsley, then stir into the mixture in the pan and leave it all to cool.

Preheat the oven to 190°C/fan 170°C/gas mark 5. Spoon the cooled filling into the hollow vegetables, filling them up about three-quarters, so there is room for the rice to expand. Lay the large cooked onion petals out in front of you and stuff those also, leaving a bit of room for growth. Tuck the edges under, so you have an 'eye' shape, and nestle them into the tray, seam side down. Dissolve the remaining tablespoon of tomato purée in the hot stock and whisk in the juice from the lemon. Pour some of the stock over the filled vegetables and the rest directly into the tray, so that it comes just over halfway up the sides of the tallest vegetables. It is important there is enough liquid, so if it is not high enough up the vegetables, top it up with hot water. Replace the tops of the vegetables, drizzle them with the remaining oil and then cover the tray with foil and place in the oven. Cook for 1 hour, then remove the foil, turn the heat up to 220°C/fan 200°C/gas mark 7 and cook for a further 20–25 minutes, until the outsides of the vegetables are slightly caramelised. You can serve these straight away, but gemista are better if left to cool a little, ideally 20–30 minutes. The flavours develop and the rice gets a chance to soak up any extra liquid in the tray. They're even nicer the next day.

(Photo overleaf)

Gemista (pages 200–1)

Dolmades

Taverna, the book of my family's Greek-Cypriot recipes, included my yiayia's *koupepia*, her version of stuffed vine leaves that contains pork mince. However, most Greek versions are vegan, and so can be eaten at any time of the year.

MAKES 45–50

4 onions
80ml olive oil
5 tomatoes
1 heaped tablespoon tomato purée
275g medium grain rice (or a mixture of short and long grain)
1 tablespoon dried mint
½ teaspoon ground cinnamon
½ teaspoon each of sea salt and freshly ground black pepper
75g pine nuts, optional
1 bunch of flat-leaf parsley
A few dill sprigs
50 vine leaves
2 lemons

Peel and finely chop the onions. Place half of the oil in a wide saucepan over a medium-low heat and soften the onions for 15 minutes. Stir them occasionally, and add a splash of water if they begin to catch. Coarsely grate in four of the tomatoes, discarding the skins. Stir in the tomato purée and keep cooking until most of the juices have reduced, and you are left with a little liquid in the bottom of the pan (this will be soaked up by the rice). Stir in the rice, dried mint, cinnamon, salt, pepper and pine nuts, if using. Finely chop the parsley and dill and add those to the pan, then turn off the heat and leave to cool.

Bring a large pan of water to the boil. In batches, blanch the vine leaves in a pan of boiling water for just a minute. Transfer to a colander, as you continue. When they are all ready, set yourself up a conveyor belt of leaves, filling and pan. To fill them, lay a leaf out in front of you, textured side facing up, with the stalk closest to you. Spoon a couple of teaspoons of the rice mixture towards the bottom of the leaf, in the centre, and roll the bottom edge of the leaf over the filling once. Fold over each side, then keep rolling until the leaf has encased the filling. The amount of mixture you use will depend on the size of the leaf. Once you start you'll find your rhythm. Repeat with all the leaves and filling.

Line the bottom of a large saucepan with any broken or leftover vine leaves. Layer up the rolled dolmades, so they are closely layered but not packed too tight (the rice will expand as it cooks). Coarsely grate the remaining tomato into 800ml of just-boiled boiled water. Squeeze in the juice from the lemons and whisk in with the remaining olive oil. Pour the seasoned water over the layered vine leaves. If they are not quite covered, add enough just-boiled water so they are just covered. Place an upturned heavy plate directly on top of the dolmades, cover the pan with a lid and place on a medium heat. Bring to a steady simmer, then reduce the heat and cook for 45 minutes, until most of the liquid has been absorbed and the dolmades are cooked through. Open one up to test – you are looking for sweet, sticky, tomatoey rice that is tender and done. Turn off the heat and leave, still covered, to rest for at least 15 minutes before serving.

Maqluba: *upside-down layer cake*

When I was writing this book, I video-called with Elham Matalka in Jordan during Lent. She told me all about her favourite dishes to eat during this time, and would then send me pictures of them as she made them. One of these dishes was called maqluba, an Arabic word that means 'upside down'. Elham eats it while fasting for Lent, but it's also a popular to eat for iftar, the evening meal that breaks the daily fast during Ramadan.

This is a 'cake' of various layers cooked on the hob in a pot. As the components slowly cook they're being gently compressed, so that when it is ready the whole thing is turned out – upside down – on a serving platter. It's a bit of a process but it isn't hard to make, and the end result is the perfect meal for a celebration or gathering. If you ever feel short-changed by vegan roast dinners, present this with a side of chopped salad, and everyone will have a feast.

I have left the rice type vague, as there are many variations, and you can use what you like or have. Elham suggests short grain, but I love a combination, one third short grain and the rest basmati – I think this gives the perfect balance of flavour and stickiness to keep the cake together.

SERVES 6

1 small cauliflower, around 450g
350g waxy potatoes, Cyprus if possible
3 red onions
Olive oil
Sea salt and freshly ground black pepper
2 teaspoons Lebanese seven-spice (see page 111 for how to make your own)
2 tablespoons pomegranate molasses
600g rice (see above)
3 large ripe tomatoes
1 large aubergine
200g vermicelli pasta or noodles
½ teaspoon dried oregano
800ml hot vegetable stock
40g pine nuts
40g flaked almonds
½ bunch of flat-leaf parsley

Preheat your oven to 220°C/fan 200°C/gas mark 7. Cut the cauliflower into even florets, halving any larger pieces. Slice the potatoes into 5mm-thick slices. Peel the onions and cut into 2cm-thick wedges. Place these all in a large roasting tray and drizzle liberally with olive oil. Season generously and sprinkle with the Lebanese seven-spice. Toss together and roast for 30 minutes, drizzling with the pomegranate molasses 5 minutes before the end, so that the vegetables lightly char and caramelise.

Meanwhile, prepare the rest of the ingredients. Boil a kettle and line a large plate and a small plate with kitchen paper. Place the rice in a large bowl and cover with just-boiled water and leave to one side. Slice the tomatoes into 1cm-thick slices. Trim the aubergines and slice into 1cm strips lengthways. Place a large frying pan on a medium heat and drizzle in enough olive oil to just cover the base of the pan. In batches, fry the aubergine for 8–10 minutes, turning halfway through and seasoning while cooking, until lightly golden all over. Transfer to the large paper-lined plate. Break the pasta (or noodles) into small pieces and place in the pan, still on a medium heat. Add another layer of oil and fry the pasta pieces for about 5 minutes, or until golden brown. Turn off the heat and transfer the pasta to the small paper-lined plate. Drain the rice in a sieve, then return to the bowl and toss through the fried vermicelli. Season with half a teaspoon each of salt and pepper.

Now, everything should be ready for you to layer up the maqluba. Line the base of a large saucepan with the fried aubergine slices, allowing them to come slightly up the side of the pan to help the maqluba maintain its structure. Next, lay over the tomato slices and sprinkle with oregano. Top with half of the roasted cauliflower and red onion wedges, arranged evenly. Place two-thirds of the rice-vermicelli mixture into the pan, patting it in to make it even. Top with the roasted potato and the remaining cauliflower and onion. Scatter over the remaining rice mixture. Pour in the hot stock. It should sit about 1cm under the level of the rice.

Put the pan on a medium heat and bring it the boil, then reduce the heat to the lowest setting. Place a thick plate, slightly smaller than the pan, on top, so that it sits directly on top of the rice, and cover the pan with a lid. Cook on a low heat for 1 hour and 15 minutes, until the rice is cooked through and the water has been absorbed. If it is not quite ready, cook for a further 10 minutes. Remove from the heat and leave to one side, still covered, for 10 minutes. Meanwhile, toast the pine nuts and flaked almonds in a small dry frying pan, stirring occasionally, over a low heat for 5 minutes, or until lightly golden. Finely chop the parsley leaves. When the maqluba has stood for 10 minutes, remove the lid and plate and place a wide, heavy platter on top of the pan. Quickly and confidently turn the pan over and give it a tap. The maqluba should turn out in one piece. Remove the pan, then scatter with the toasted nuts and parsley before taking to the table.

(Photo overleaf)

Maqluba (pages 206–7)

Spanakorizo: *sweet and smoky spinach, tomato and lemon rice*

This is a classic Lenten Greek dish, and can be as simple or elaborate as you like. Simplicity can be wonderful but I do like to add a few more ingredients to my spanakorizo; then I'm not reliant on the flavour from super-sweet summer tomatoes and it becomes a year-round dinner. I love how the subtle (and it is subtle, I promise) smokiness from a little smoked salt complements the sweet smoked paprika. However, if you can't get hold of smoked salt, of course it is still delicious with regular salt.

SERVES 4

2 onions
2 garlic cloves
1 leek
4 spring onions
75ml olive oil
1 heaped teaspoon smoked or regular flaky salt
400g spinach
200g long grain rice
2 tablespoons tomato purée
1 heaped teaspoon sugar
¼ teaspoon sweet smoked paprika
350ml tomato passata or 5 ripe tomatoes
750ml vegetable stock
Freshly ground black pepper
1 lemon
½ bunch of dill

Start by peeling and chopping the onions and garlic cloves. Trim and finely slice the leek and give it a thorough rinse in a colander to get rid of any dirt. Trim and slice the spring onions into 1cm pieces. Place the olive oil in a large saucepan over a medium-low heat. Add the chopped vegetables and smoked (or regular) salt and sauté for 15 minutes, until softened and sticky but not coloured. Meanwhile, really thoroughly wash the spinach – the last thing you want is grit in the spinach, so my yiayia always washes hers three times! When it is grit-free, roughly chop and leave to one side. Rinse the rice in a sieve under running water for minute.

When the vegetables are ready, stir in the tomato purée, sugar and sweet smoked paprika. Fry for a few minutes, then stir in the washed rice and cook for a further minute. Add the passata (or coarsely grate in the tomatoes, discarding the skin) and the stock, then season with a few pinches of pepper. Turn the heat up and bring to the boil. Once it is bubbling, stir in the chopped spinach, then cover with the lid and reduce the heat to low. Cook for 30 minutes, stirring once halfway through and adding more water if it looks like the rice has dried out and is sticking to the bottom of the pan. After half an hour, the rice should be cooked; give it a stir and check the texture – it should feel like a paella. If it is a little on the wet side, cook with the lid off to reduce it. Remember the rice will absorb liquid as it cools, so don't reduce the liquid too much. Squeeze in the lemon juice, taste and tweak the seasoning, then leave for 5 minutes before serving. Finely chop the dill and scatter over the rice. Serve warm.

5 *Cakes, biscuits and puddings*

Traditionally most sweet treats were out of bounds during fasting periods – vegan or otherwise. It is a time to reflect and strip back, not to celebrate and behave lavishly. However, you do find recipes for Lenten cakes in old books and even on the Mount Athos website, so it isn't entirely inappropriate to include this chapter. However, puddings and cakes are still seen as very much a treat during Lent and other fasts, and should be treated as such – no dessert every day, I'm afraid. Biscuits are viewed with slightly more leniency, and most homes will have a tin of homemade cookies that last the duration. Other favourites for a sweet lift in the afternoon include tahini halva, which is intense, sweet and sustaining – you don't need a lot, so it is a perfect fasting snack. Making your own will earn you all the yiayia brownie points.

Milopita: *apple, brown sugar and cinnamon cake*

I adore an apple pie and cake. This Greek classic is one of the first sweet things I ever learned to make with my mum – it's a recipe passed down from her mum, to her from her mum, and so on. *Pita* usually refers to a pie, but to say this is a pie – or even a cake – in the English sense of the word is misleading. Somewhere in between, it is best served fresh and warm, with a dollop of something creamy (vegan or dairy, whatever works for you).

SERVES 8

4 eating apples
Juice of ½ lemon, or a splash of brandy
200g light soft brown sugar
275g self-raising flour
1 teaspoon baking powder
100g ground almonds
2 teaspoons ground cinnamon
¼ teaspoon fine sea salt
200ml vegetable oil, plus extra for the tin
150ml almond milk
1 teaspoon vanilla extract
40g mixed nuts (walnuts, hazelnuts, almonds)
Icing sugar, to finish

Preheat your oven to 190°C/fan 170°C/gas mark 5. Peel the apples and cut into quarters. Remove the core then finely slice the flesh. Place the apple slices in a large bowl, and toss with the lemon juice (or brandy) and 175g of the light soft brown sugar and leave for 5 minutes. Add the self-raising flour, baking powder, ground almonds, ground cinnamon and sea salt. Toss to combine, then add the vegetable oil, almond milk and vanilla, then mix together. Grease a 24cm round dish with a little oil. Spoon in the apple cake mixture. Roughly chop the nuts, then sprinkle them over the top with the remaining 25g of sugar. Place in the oven and bake for 40–45 minutes, or until golden and just cooked through. Dust with sifted icing sugar and leave to cool for 10 minutes before serving.

Sticky chocolate-orange pudding

This is one of the more surprising recipes in the book – it sounds very modern but is based on an old Greek recipe for chocolate and tahini cake. The self-saucing element is my contemporary twist. Make it for your most chocolate-eating, traditional dessert-loving friends – I guarantee, no one will know it is *nistisimo*.

SERVES 6–8

80ml vegetable oil, plus extra for the tin
250g caster sugar
130g plain flour
2 teaspoons baking powder
55g cocoa powder
¼ teaspoon fine sea salt
3 oranges, or 1 orange and 125ml orange juice
1 teaspoon vanilla extract
75g light soft brown sugar
Icing sugar, to finish

To serve: Ice-cream, cream or yoghurt, dairy-free or regular

Preheat your oven to 200°C/fan 180°C/gas mark 6. Grease a deep oval 25cm ceramic dish with a little oil.

In a large mixing bowl whisk together 150g of the caster sugar, the plain flour, the baking powder, 30g of the cocoa powder and the fine sea salt. Finely grate in the zest of one of the oranges and then whisk the dry ingredients all together. Finely grate, or pare and finely slice, the zest from another orange, and set aside. Squeeze the oranges into a jug to get 125ml of orange juice (alternatively, use 125ml of fresh orange juice). Whisk the vegetable oil and vanilla extract into the juice. Mix the wet mixture into the dry ingredients. Spoon the batter into the prepared baking dish and even out across the top. Put a kettle of water on to boil. In a medium mixing bowl, combine the light soft brown sugar with the remaining 100g of caster sugar and 25g of cocoa. Sprinkle this chocolate-sugar evenly over the chocolate sponge mixture. Pour 300ml of just-boiled water over the top and then pop the baking dish in the oven. Bake for 35–40 minutes, until set on top, then remove from the oven and leave to one side for 15 minutes. Sift over icing sugar and sprinkle with the reserved orange zest. Serve straight up, or with a dairy-free ice-cream, cream or yoghurt – whichever is your favourite!

Phanouropita: *the lost and found cake of Saint Phanourios*

In the Orthodox church, St Phanourios is the saint of lost things – the verb *phanerono* means 'to reveal' – and this cake is made whenever he is asked for help finding things, or people. It is most often eaten in thanks on his memorial day, 27th August. It is made the night before, then taken to church in the morning for a blessing. Once it has been blessed, the phanouropita is cut into forty pieces, symbolising the forty days of the soul in purgatory, and should then be shared with the congregation, friends and family – at least seven people should partake. It is said that sharing pieces of phanouropita will help unmarried women find a husband, help people find the right path in life and help farmers find stolen or lost animals. What a cake!

You'll find recipe variations, but orange is a key ingredient, as is olive oil, as phanouropita is always a fasting cake. Traditionally, it also would feature seven or nine ingredients to symbolise the days of creation or seven or nine Mysteries of the Greek Orthodox Church (depending on the scripture of different churches). I have adapted my family's recipe to include ground walnuts, which bring a little more moisture to the cake. Even so, this is a relatively crumbly cake, subtly lovely and perfect with a coffee in the afternoon.

SERVES 16

250ml light olive oil or other flavourless oil, plus extra for the tin
200g walnuts, plus extra, optional, for decorating
200g caster sugar
4 oranges or 1 orange and 250ml orange juice
300g self-raising flour
1 teaspoon baking powder
1 teaspoon ground cinnamon
100g raisins
125g icing sugar

Preheat your oven to 190°C/fan 170°C/gas mark 5. Grease a 24cm round cake tin with a little oil and line the base with greaseproof paper. Finely chop 75g of the walnuts and keep to one side. Grind the rest in a food processor or spice grinder until fine. In a large mixing bowl, whisk together the caster sugar with the oil until smooth. Finely grate in the zest of one orange. Squeeze all the oranges into a jug until you have 250ml juice, then whisk it into the oil and sugar mixture. Add the ground walnuts and sift in the self-raising flour, baking powder and ground cinnamon. Fold in the dry ingredients with a metal spoon, then stir in the raisins and chopped walnuts. Pour the batter into the prepared tin and bake for 40–45 minutes, or until cooked through. Cool in the tin for 10 minutes then transfer to a wire cooling rack.

Sift the icing sugar into a small mixing bowl and add just enough orange juice or water to make a thick but drizzle consistency icing – a couple of tablespoons should be enough. Drizzle over the cooled cake and decorate as you wish, with some grated orange zest, walnuts, candied orange peel or leave simply as is.

Helbeh: *fenugreek cake*

Chef Sami Tamimi first introduced me to helbeh. I was heavily pregnant with my youngest and batch cooking in anticipation of her arrival, and he suggested making it as fenugreek is said to aid milk production. Until then, I'd only ever used fenugreek seeds in curries and other savoury dishes. I didn't manage to make it before Elektra's arrival, but this intriguing cake came up when I was speaking to Elham Matalka about Jordanian fasting food. With slightly more time on my hands, I gave it a go – now it's one of my favourite cakes in the book. The fenugreek seeds are boiled to soften their bitterness (you may get a little bitter bite but it isn't unpleasant), leaving the most beguiling, almost floral flavour. There isn't anything quite like it. If you can, make this a day ahead of when you want to serve it, so the flavours really develop.

MAKES 40 PIECES

280g caster sugar
½ lemon
2 tablespoons orange blossom water, optional
15g fenugreek seeds
2 tablespoons tahini
350g fine semolina
100g plain flour
90ml olive oil
½ teaspoon aniseed
½ × 7g sachet of fast-action dried yeast
½ teaspoon baking powder
½ teaspoon ground cinnamon
½ teaspoon fine sea salt
40 blanched almonds, optional

Start by making the syrup. Place the caster sugar in a small pan with 375ml of water, the juice of the lemon half and the orange blossom water, if using. Bring to the boil over a high heat, then reduce the heat a little and leave to bubble away for about 8 minutes. You want this to be syrupy but not golden. When it is done, turn off the heat and leave to one side to cool completely. In another small pan, bring the fenugreek seeds to the boil in 500ml of water, and simmer over a medium heat until the water has reduced by about half. Leave this to cool completely also.

When the syrup and steeped fenugreek seeds are cold you can prepare the cake. Grease a 24cm round tin with the tahini. Whisk together the semolina and plain flour in a large mixing bowl. Add the olive oil and rub it into the dry ingredients until evenly mixed in, like breadcrumbs.

Grind the aniseed in a pestle and mortar and add to the mixing bowl along with the dried yeast, baking powder, ground cinnamon and fine sea salt. Stir everything together. Strain the cooked fenugreek seeds, reserving the liquid. Add the seeds to the bowl, along with 225ml of the cooking water. Mix it all together. Don't overmix it, you just want it to come together – add one or two tablespoons more of the water if needed. Pat the dough into the greased tin and cut into diamonds – if you do about 40, this should make the pieces a good size. Pop an almond into each diamond, if using. Leave to one side for 1 hour, to prove a little.

Preheat your oven to 200°C/fan 180°C/gas mark 6. Bake the cake for 30–35 minutes, until golden. As soon as it is ready, evenly pour over the cooled syrup and leave the helbeh to cool. Do not cut this for at least 1 hour, but the longer you can leave it (overnight if possible), the better.

Hareeseh: *Jordanian coconut semolina cake*

You will find variations of syrupy semolina tray bakes across the Mediterranean and Middle East. In Cyprus we call it *shamali* (or *kalon prama* which translates as 'good thing' – I find this particularly pleasing). In Greece and Turkey it is *revani*, in Egypt it is *basbousa*, in Lebanon it is *namoura*, and in Jordan it is *hareeseh*. They're all similar, but not the same, and I particularly love the gentle coconuttiness that runs through hareeseh. To adapt this for fasting, I simply switched the traditional yoghurt to a dairy-free coconut version. The key points here are that the cake shouldn't be too thick or the pieces too big, as it will all become too crumbly, and you want a nice, evenly golden top to act like a binding crust and help keep it all together.

MAKES 30 PIECES

340g caster sugar
½ lemon
1 tablespoon orange blossom water
1 tablespoon rose water
125ml vegetable or light olive oil, plus extra for the tin
300g regular semolina
50g desiccated coconut
½ tablespoon baking powder
200g dairy-free coconut yoghurt
30 almonds, to decorate

Start by making the syrup, as this needs to be completely cold when the cake is ready. Place 225g of the caster sugar in a small pan with 350ml of water and the juice from the lemon half. Bring to the boil over a medium heat, then reduce the heat a little and simmer for 10 minutes. Stir in the orange blossom and rose water and leave to one side to cool completely.

Preheat your oven to 200°C/fan 180°C/gas mark 6. Brush a 23 × 33cm roasting tin or 30–31cm circular tin with a little olive oil. In a large bowl, mix together the semolina, desiccated coconut, baking powder and the remaining 115g of caster sugar. Whisk together, then make a well and pour in the vegetable or olive oil. Mix it in with a fork so that every grain gets coated in oil, then mix in the coconut yoghurt. Mix together until combined – it will be a thick mixture. Spoon the mixture into the greased tin (you don't want it to be more than 2.5cm thick) and gently score the top into small diamond shapes, about 3–4cm. Place a blanched almond into the centre of each piece and place the tin in the oven. Bake for 40–45 minutes, or until the top is golden brown.

When the cake comes out of the oven, slowly and evenly pour over the cooled syrup. Leave to soak in for at least 2 hours before serving.

Ghapama loaf cake

Sharice Babakhani, my go-to for Armenian fasting food, told me about ghapama, a recipe that is popular in the lead-up to Christmas. It's a striking dish: a whole pumpkin stuffed with rice, spices, nuts and honey-drenched dried fruit, then baked. I was inspired to channel those flavours into a loaf cake that could be enjoyed year-round, but would be especially appealing during the cooler months when pumpkins are available. However, if you are making this in spring or summer, you can use tinned pumpkin purée, or puréed butternut squash.

SERVES 8–10

- 100g dairy-free spread, plus a little extra for the tin
- 100g raisins, dried apple or apricots, or a mixture
- 275g light soft brown sugar
- 75ml orange or apple juice
- 150g pumpkin purée, homemade or tinned
- 2 tablespoons honey (or maple syrup)
- 1 teaspoon vanilla extract
- 165g plain flour
- 2 teaspoons baking powder
- 1½ teaspoons ground cinnamon
- ¼ teaspoon ground cloves
- ¼ teaspoon salt
- 30g nuts (I like to use almonds, pistachios, walnuts)
- Gold leaf, for decorating, optional

Grease and line a large loaf tin with greaseproof paper. If using dried apple or apricots, chop them into small pieces, around 1–2cm. Place all the dried fruit into a pan with 75g of the light soft brown sugar, 25g of the dairy-free spread and all the juice. Bring to a boil over a medium heat. Swirl the pan to help melt the sugar, then reduce the heat a little and leave to bubble gently away for 6–8 minutes, swirling the pan a few more times. When you have a thick, deep-golden syrup, remove the pan from the heat. Pour the syrup and fruit into the bottom of the lined loaf tin and leave to one side.

Preheat your oven to 190°C/fan 170°C/gas mark 5. Melt the remaining 75g of dairy-free spread. Place it in a large mixing bowl with the remaining 200g of light soft brown sugar and the pumpkin purée, honey and vanilla extract. Stir in four tablespoons of water and mix until smooth. Sift in the flour, baking powder, spices and salt, then fold into the wet mixture. When everything has just come together, spoon the batter into the lined tin and pop in the oven. Bake for 40–50 minutes, until golden and cooked through. Leave the cake in the tin to cool for 5 minutes before turning out onto a cooling rack. Chop the nuts and scatter over the cake. Leave to cool completely, then decorate with the gold leaf, if you like, and serve.

Pivčići: *apricot, beer and walnut rolls*

A fabulous woman called Kristina Vučinić taught me several Serbian fasting recipes, and this is one of her favourites. These little biscuits are surprisingly easy and very fun to make and really rather addictive to eat – unusual and not too sweet. It's also a very adaptable recipe, if you want to play around with the types of jam and nuts.

MAKES 32

250g self-raising flour, plus extra for dusting
1½ teaspoons baking powder
A pinch of salt
100ml sunflower oil
100ml beer
60g apricot jam
150g caster sugar
½ lemon
100g walnuts

Preheat your oven to 190°C/fan 170°C/gas mark 5. In a mixing bowl, whisk together the self-raising flour, baking powder and salt and make a well in the centre. Pour in the sunflower oil and beer and whisk until a dough is formed. Knead for a minute then turn out onto a lightly floured surface. Divide the dough equally in two and roll each piece into a ball. Place the balls of dough between sheets of greaseproof paper and roll out into circles that are 2mm thick – it is important that they are circular. Cut each circle in half, then quarters and so on, until you have 16 triangles (32 in total). Spoon a small amount of jam onto the wide end of each triangle and start rolling the little rolls, from wide end in. Line baking trays with greaseproof paper – you can use the sheets you used to roll the dough – and evenly space out the little rolls. Pop the trays in the oven and bake for 15–18 minutes, swapping the trays part-way through if they're cooking unevenly. When the rolls are done, they should be just golden.

While the rolls are baking, make the syrup. Place the sugar in a medium saucepan with 100ml of water and the juice from the lemon half. Bring to the boil, reduce the heat to low and simmer for 5 minutes. Grind the walnuts using a spice grinder or pestle and mortar – avoid using a food processor, if possible, as a bit of texture is needed here, and the walnuts go oily if they break down too much.

When the rolls are baked, pop them straight in the pan with the syrup. Do this in batches. Use tongs to turn them, and leave them in for less than a minute. You want them syrupy enough that the nuts stick , but not so soaked as to be soggy. Use the tongs to retrieve them from the syrup, roll in the ground walnuts and place on a tray. Keep going until all the biscuits are coated. Leave until cool before eating, and store any left over in an airtight container.

Melomakarona: *spiced honey biscuits*

It's a good idea to make these traditional Greek Christmas biscuits ahead of the busiest festive cooking days as, thanks to being plunged in a preserving sugar syrup, they last incredibly well. In my book of family recipes, *Taverna*, I shared my yiayia's recipe, which includes eggs. My *nistisimo* version is just as delicious, and means that we can eat them when we're fasting ahead of Christmas.

MAKES 25 OR SO

500g plain flour, plus a little extra, if needed
1 teaspoon baking powder
½ teaspoon bicarbonate of soda
2 teaspoons ground cinnamon
1 teaspoon mixed spice
½ teaspoon fine sea salt
250g caster sugar
235ml olive oil
100ml orange juice
2 tablespoons brandy
150ml honey, plus extra for drizzling
1 cinnamon stick
75g walnuts

Preheat the oven to 180°C/fan 160°C/gas mark 4. Line two baking sheets with greaseproof paper. Sift the flour into a large mixing bowl, along with the baking powder, bicarbonate of soda, ground cinnamon, mixed spice and salt, then add 100g of the sugar. Make a well in the middle of the dry ingredients and pour in the olive oil, orange juice and brandy. Mix it all together, initially with a fork, then with your hands until it is combined and smooth. If the mixture feels a little greasy, add a little more flour, but only just enough to bring it together; it shouldn't be too stiff.

Roll the dough into golf ball-sized pieces, and shape them slightly into an oblong shape. Space them out evenly on the lined baking sheets and place in the oven. Bake for 20–25 minutes, until golden.

Meanwhile, make the syrup. Place the honey in a small pan with the remaining 150g of caster sugar, 400ml of water and the cinnamon stick. Bring to the boil over a medium heat, then reduce to a simmer and leave to gently bubble for 6–8 minutes, until thickened. Finely chop the walnuts and keep to one side.

When the biscuits are ready, leave to cool for 10 minutes, then carefully dip each one into the warm honey syrup until completely coated. I do about four at a time and leave them in for about 30 seconds on each side. You don't want to do too many at once, because you don't want them to go soggy. Transfer the dipped melomakarona to a board, drizzle with a tiny bit more honey and sprinkle with the chopped walnuts. Leave to cool before serving, or store in an airtight container where they should keep nicely for at least a week.

(Photo overleaf)

Tahinobiskoto: *tahini, almond and honey cookies*

In the canon of store-cupboard bakes, this is the *most* store-cupboard thing I have ever come up with: these cookies consist of very few ingredients and come together in next to no time. Think of these as Greek amaretti (the soft chewy kind) and you are on the right track. If you can get hold of black sesame seeds then use a mixture as it looks striking. If not, don't worry as it doesn't make a noticeable difference to the flavour.

MAKES 12

150g ground almonds
1 teaspoon baking powder
¼ teaspoon fine sea salt
100g tahini
90g honey
15g sesame seeds, a mixture of black and white, ideally

Preheat your oven to 180°C/fan 160°C/gas mark 4. Line two baking sheets with greaseproof paper. Whisk together the ground almonds, baking powder and sea salt. Add the tahini and honey and beat together until smooth. Place the sesame seeds in a bowl or on a small plate. Divide the mixture into 12 and roll into balls in your hand. Roll each ball lightly in the sesame seeds and place on the lined baking sheet. Leave a good few centimetres between them as they can spread. Press down a little on each ball to flatten slightly. Bake in the oven for 8–10 minutes, or until the biscuits are lightly golden around the edge. Leave to cool on the tray for 5 minutes then transfer to a cooling rack.

(Photo overleaf)

Moustokouloura: *spiced grape, honey and chocolate biscuits*

Along with honey and carob syrup, grape molasses is one of the oldest sweeteners used in Greek cooking. While these are all still sugars, I do feel slightly virtuous when I eat a treat that is free from refined sugar. I also love how simple these crisp biscuits are – perfect for a children's baking afternoon. They're not a traditional Christmas biscuit, but the subtle spices have a festive, warming feel and they make wonderful presents.

MAKES 36–40

500g plain flour
1 teaspoon baking powder
1 teaspoon bicarbonate of soda
1 tablespoon ground cinnamon
¼ teaspoon ground cloves
¼ teaspoon fine sea salt
175ml petimezi (grape molasses)
125ml light olive or vegetable oil, plus extra for greasing
5 tablespoons honey
2 tablespoons orange juice
150g dark chocolate
50g toasted sesame seeds or hazelnuts
Flaky sea salt

In a large mixing bowl whisk together the plain flour, baking powder, bicarbonate of soda, ground cinnamon, ground cloves and fine salt and leave to one side. In the bowl of a free-standing mixer, using a beater attachment, mix together the petimezi, oil, honey and orange juice. When the liquids are completely combined, add half the dry ingredients and combine using the beater attachment (you can also do this by hand). Add the remaining flour mixture, and mix together just enough to bring it together. Turn it out onto a lightly oiled worktop, and leave to rest for 30 minutes.

Preheat your oven to 190°C/fan 170°C/gas mark 5 and line two baking sheets with greaseproof paper. Divine the dough in half, then half again. Split each quarter into nine or 10 small balls. Roll a ball of dough into a sausage about 12cm long, then join the ends to form a circle or roll into a swirl, then place on a lined baking sheet. Continue with all the dough. Bake for about 13–15 minutes, or until just lightly golden, then leave to cool on the trays for 10 minutes, before transferring to a cooling rack.

When the biscuits have cooled, break up the chocolate into small, even pieces and melt in the microwave or in a heatproof bowl set over a pan of simmering water. Stir until glossy and smooth. Place the toasted sesame seeds in a bowl (if using hazelnuts, chop them very finely first). Half dip a biscuit into the melted chocolate then sprinkle with the sesame seeds or chopped hazelnuts and a little pinch of flaky sea salt. Transfer to a cooling rack to set, then repeat with all of the biscuits.

Top row, left: tahinobiskoto (page 231)
Middle rows, left: melomakarona (page 230)
Bottom row, left: moustokouloura (opposite)

Mama's halva

This is one of my mum's classic recipes, and for me it is one of the most nostalgic and familiar dishes in this book. She would always make it for big family gatherings, and now she makes for my cousin Cassie's birthday – it's her favourite thing in the world and her one request every year. Not to be confused with sesame halva (page 236), this halva is a set semolina sweet that looks like a cake but is more like a pudding in texture. It is super popular during fasting times, the kind of thing we eat with coffee in the afternoon rather than after dinner. The key to its super-caramelly, nutty flavour is to lightly toast the semolina before adding the sugar syrup (but not so much that it becomes bitter). If you don't want to use almond milk you can make it with water – it is still delicious.

SERVES 16

600ml almond milk
360g caster sugar
2 tablespoons orange blossom water
5 cloves
2 cinnamon sticks
1 orange
200ml sunflower or other flavourless oil, plus extra for the tin
140g blanched almonds
400g semolina (not fine)
Ground cinnamon, for sprinkling

Place the almond milk in a medium pan with 600ml of water, the caster sugar, orange blossom water, cloves and cinnamon sticks. Finely grate in the zest from the orange. Bring to the boil over a medium heat, then reduce the heat a little and simmer for 12–15 minutes, until lightly syrupy. Fish out the spices and set the syrup to one side.

Brush a medium bundt tin with a little oil. Chop the almonds, not too finely. Place the oil in a large pan over a medium-low heat. Warm it through for a minute then stir in the semolina. Toast the semolina for 5 minutes, until it turns golden – don't let it get too dark or it will become bitter. Stir in the chopped almonds and gradually add the spiced syrup to the semolina. Keep stirring and when the syrup is all in, reduce the heat to low. As soon as the mixture starts bubbling, pour it into the greased tin. Chill in the fridge overnight to set. When you're ready to serve the halva, cover the bundt tin with a large plate or platter and invert to turn out, then sprinkle liberally with ground cinnamon.

Pistachio and cardamom halva

If you visit a Greek Orthodox person's home during Lent, you're almost certain to find a slab of tahini halva on the counter, ready to slice whenever a sugar hit is needed. I love all the flavour combinations: straight-up sesame, or with chocolate, but pistachio is my absolute favourite. You don't have to add cardamom to it, most people don't, but this is my nod to the vast amount of varying sweets named halva – it is a term that spreads from Eastern Europe, through the Middle East and over to western Asia, where the Indian cardamom-laced versions are some of my all-time favourite foods.

SERVES 10–12

Olive oil
50g pistachios
8 cardamom pods
250g tahini
½ teaspoon good-quality vanilla extract
½ teaspoon fine sea salt
230g caster sugar

Grease a loaf tin with a little oil then line it with cling film, leaving some overhanging the edges of the tin. Roughly chop the pistachios. Remove the cardamom seeds from the pods, discard the pods and grind the seeds until fine. Add to a large mixing bowl with 30g of the chopped pistachios, the tahini, vanilla and sea salt and beat until smooth.

Place the sugar and 75ml of water in a medium saucepan and gently bring to the boil over a medium heat. Gently swirl the pan, do not stir the syrup or the sugar will crystallise. Once it starts to bubble, reduce the heat to low and leave to simmer for around 12–15 minutes, until you have a thick syrup. If you have a sugar thermometer, it needs to reach 121°C. When it is ready, add the tahini mixture to the pan (you don't want the mixture to cool down, it needs to stay in the warm pan) and quickly beat the two elements together to make a smooth paste. This is best done with a wooden spoon or spatula. Try not to overwork it, though, as this will make the halva crumbly – you only want to beat it for 30 seconds. As soon as it is smoothly combined, spoon it into the lined tin and press on the remaining pistachios. Leave to cool. Once cool, cover with the cling film edges and transfer to the fridge to set overnight before serving.

Mahalepi and mahalabia

Cornflour puddings feature throughout the eastern Mediterranean and Middle East in various guises: they can be water-, milk- or cream-based; use sugar or syrup as sweetener; and they tend to be floral in flavour, with nuts as a garnish. Think of them as blancmange meets panna cotta, but more fragrant, and you're on the right track. I think the rose-scented ones are more seductive and intense, while the orange blossom-laced versions seem a little gentler and more delicate. There is a place in my heart for all of them – even divisive mahalepi, the water-based Cypriot variety that is essentially a vehicle for triantaphyllo, our head-spinningly sweet rose syrup.

Mahalepi

To eat this like a true Cypriot, my advice is to go hard with the garnish. You need at least two tablespoons of triantaphyllo for each serving, do not be shy, plus extra sugar and ice-cold water. It sounds like a lot, because it is. It's not for everyone but on a hot, *hot* summer day there is nothing better.

SERVES 6

7 tablespoons niseste (see page 285) or cornflour
3 tablespoons caster sugar, plus extra to serve
3 tablespoons rose water, plus extra to serve
Ice cubes

To serve: Triantaphyllo (rose syrup, see page 286)

Mix enough water into the niseste (or cornflour) to make it into a loose paste – a few tablespoons should do it. Mix in three tablespoons of caster sugar and the rose water and leave to one side. In a medium saucepan, bring 1 litre of water to a simmer over a medium heat and pour in the rosewater paste. Whisk until it starts to bubble, then reduce the heat a little and cook for about 5 minutes, until you have a thick mixture. Rinse six small bowls under a cold tap and leave to one side; it's important to keep them wet. When you're happy that your mixture is smooth and thickened, pour into your bowls and leave to cool. As soon as they have cooled down, transfer to the fridge and leave to set overnight.

Once the mahalepi has set firm add a few tablespoons of cold water to each bowl, to keep the puddings from drying out. Alternatively, slide the round puddings into one larger dish, and cover with lots of cold water. They last happily in there, and take up less room in the fridge. Serve the mahalepi in bowls, roughtly diced and topped with a ladle of the chilled water, a tablespoon or so of caster sugar, an extra teaspoon of rose water, and a good spoonful of triantaphyllo drizzled on top. If it is really warm outside, add a couple of extra ice cubes.

(Photo overleaf)

Mahalabia

If you are not averse to using dairy-free cream, feel free to replace half the almond milk with it for a richer pudding.

SERVES 6–8

7 tablespoons cornflour
1 litre almond milk
275g caster sugar
1 tablespoon orange blossom water
½ lemon
1 tablespoon rose water
40g pistachios
25g flaked almonds

Place the cornflour in a mixing bowl and whisk in enough almond milk to make a smooth paste. Pour the remaining milk into a large saucepan with 75g of the caster sugar and warm over a medium heat. When it starts to bubble, whisk in the cornflour mixture, and keep whisking. Lower the heat and cook over a lower heat for around 5–8 minutes, still whisking, until thickened and glossy. Stir in the orange blossom water and then pour or ladle into 6–8 serving bowls. Leave to cool then transfer to the fridge to set.

Meanwhile, make the syrup. Place the remaining 200g of caster sugar in a pan with 250ml of water and the juice from the lemon half. Bring to the boil over a high heat, then reduce to a simmer and leave to bubble away for 8–10 minutes until lightly syrupy but not golden. Stir in the rose water and leave to cool, then transfer to a jug.

When you are ready to serve, roughly chop the pistachios and decorate the puddings with the chopped and flaked nuts. Serve with the jug syrup on the side, for people to pour over according to their taste.

Above: mahalepi (page 238)

Erene's rizogalo: *rose rice pudding with roasted strawberries*

It was a grey day in early March, Greek Easter Lent had just started and I was playing in the kitchen developing a *nistisimo* rizogalo (literally translated as 'rice milk'). There was a knock on the door, and it was Erene Panteli – my neighbour and one of the chefs at our neighbourhood Greek-Cypriot deli. A few days previously, I had been interviewing her for this book (her locally famous vegan keftedes feature on page 150) – and now she had a container in her hand. 'I thought you might like to try my vegan rizogalo,' she said. Erene's non-Lenten rizogalo is much-loved around these parts, so yes, I did want to try it. And my goodness, it was heaven; it had to be included.

Erene uses drinking coconut milk, as opposed to the stuff you get in a tin, and it does make a particularly fine rizogalo. However, use whatever you can get; oat or almond milk would be good. I serve this with roasted strawberries to cut through the creaminess – even though this rizogalo is *nistisimo* it is still rich. It is also lovely with macerated fresh berries, or simply as it is.

SERVES 4

750ml non-dairy milk, ideally coconut
160g pudding rice
150g granulated sugar
2 tablespoons rose water
1 tablespoon vanilla extract
250ml non-dairy cream
½–1 teaspoon ground cinnamon
300g strawberries
½ lemon

Place the milk and rice in a large heavy-bottomed saucepan, then add 100g granulated sugar, one tablespoon of rose water and half the vanilla extract. Bring to the boil over a medium heat, give it a good stir, then reduce the heat to low and cook for 25–30 minutes, stirring occasionally, until the rice is perfectly cooked – just tender and creamy. Stir in the cream, warming through for 1 minute, then remove from the heat. Ladle into serving bowls, or one large bowl, and sprinkle liberally with the ground cinnamon. You can serve this now, or leave it to cool and then chill in the fridge, as is traditional.

For the strawberries, preheat your oven to 220°C/fan 200°C/gas mark 7. Hull the strawberries and halve any larger ones. Place the berries in a snug fitting roasting tray and toss with the remaining 50g of granulated sugar. Squeeze over the lemon juice, and add the remaining one tablespoon of rose water and half a tablespoon of vanilla extract. Mix together well and place the tray in the oven. Roast for 15–20 minutes, until the strawberries are tender but not mushy. Like the rizogalo, the strawberries are lovely served warm or chilled, just spoon them (and some of the juices from the tray) over a bowl of the creamy pudding.

Anthous: *deep-fried flowers, honey and pistachio*

We think of elderflower as a real taste of British spring and summer, but elders are found all over Cyprus and the blossoms are frequently used in home remedies. During the elderflower and courgette flower seasons, I've often seen my yiayias and aunts turn the delicate blooms into light fritters, drizzled with honey. I've embellished the recipe slightly with a little crushed fennel in the batter, as it works beautifully with the gentle nature of the flowers.

SERVES 4

2 pinches of fine sea salt
½ teaspoon fennel seeds
130g plain flour
1 teaspoon caster sugar
¼ teaspoon fast-action dried yeast
300ml cold sparkling water
1 litre vegetable oil
20g pistachios
12 courgette flowers or elderflower heads
3 tablespoons honey (agave or maple syrup will work well here)

Place a pinch of salt and the fennel seeds in a mortar and grind with the pestle until you have a fine powder. Place into a large bowl with the plain flour, caster sugar and dried yeast and whisk to combine. Slowly whisk in the sparkling water, until smooth, adding a splash more water if needed to reach a double-cream consistency. Then whisk in another pinch of salt. Cover the bowl with a tea towel and leave to one side.

Place the vegetable oil in a large saucepan on a medium heat. Place a small cube of bread or potato in the oil; when it turns golden-brown the oil is ready. Meanwhile, finely chop the pistachios. Trim the flowers, removing the stamen if using courgette flowers. Then when the oil is ready and you are ready to fry, dip the flowers in the batter, let the excess drip off, then carefully lower into the hot oil. You may need to do this in batches. Fry the flowers for 1–2 minutes, until golden and crisp, then transfer to a plate lined with kitchen paper to absorb any excess oil. Drizzle the hot fritters with honey, scatter with the chopped pistachios and serve immediately.

Ekmek: *kataifi milk pie*

My yiayia and I both love millk-based puddings, and I first made a vegan version of this Greek classic when she was fasting and in need of a sweet treat. Although we both thought it utterly delicious, I don't often adapt milk-based recipes using dairy alternatives, so wasn't sure if I'd include it here. However, during my research I discovered that the monks of Mount Athos also make a *nistisimo* version of ekmek, also using dairy alternatives, and I figured if it's good enough for the Mount Athos monks, then it's OK to feature it here.

SERVES 8

375g caster sugar
1 cinnamon stick
3 cloves
5 tablespoons light olive or vegetable oil
200g kataifi pastry
10 tbsp cornflour
1.25 litres almond milk
2 tablespoons orange blossom water
2 tablespoons rose water
40g nuts, I like pistachio and almonds
Rose petals and gold leaf, optional, to decorate

Start by making the syrup so it has time to cool. Place 250g of the caster sugar in a small pan with 300ml of water, the cinnamon stick and cloves, and bring to the boil over a high heat. Once bubbling, reduce to a medium heat and leave to gently bubble away for around 6–8 minutes, until syrupy but not coloured. Leave to one side to cool completely. When cool, preheat your oven to 200°C/fan 180°C/gas mark 6. Brush a 24cm square cake tin with a little oil. Tease the kataifi into the bottom of the tin, then drizzle over the oil. Toss it through the pastry, then spread out the kataifi so it evenly covers the base. Bake in the oven for 20–25 minutes, or until evenly golden. Remove from the oven and evenly pour the cooled sugar syrup all over the pastry, discarding the spices. Leave to one side to cool.

When the pastry is cool, make the milk layer. Place the cornflour in a large mixing bowl and whisk in just enough of the almond milk to form a smooth paste – six tablespoons should be enough. Place the remaining almond milk and 125g caster sugar in a large pan and gently bring to the boil over a medium heat. Ladle a little hot milk into the cornflour mixture, whisk it in till smooth, then pour the cornflour-milk mixture into the pan with the rest of the milk and whisk together until well combined. Keep whisking over the heat until you feel the milk thicken, then reduce the heat a little, and add the orange blossom and rose waters. Keep whisking until you have a smooth custard that thickly coats the back of a spoon – this should take about 4–5 minutes. Pour the fragrant custard over the soaked and cooled kataifi pastry. Then it's time to decorate. Roughly chop the nuts and scatter them over, along with some rose petals. I even like to add a little gold leaf once the custard has cooled. Once the ekmek has cooled completely, transfer it to the fridge for at least 4 hours, to allow it to set before serving.

Roasted cherry and tarragon hand pies

Pirozhki translates from Russian as 'little pies', but because they're usually made with a yeasted dough, they are perhaps closer to what we think of as buns. They can be sweet or savoury, and are easily made into vegan versions. I've shallow fried these, as I think they are more delicious, but there is no reason why you can't bake them. Preheat your oven to 210°C/fan 190°C/gas mark 6½ and bake for around 20 minutes until golden. Make sure to give them a little lemony glaze at the end.

MAKES 12

- 500g strong white bread flour, plus extra for dusting
- ¾ teaspoon fine sea salt
- ½ × 7g sachet of fast-action dried yeast
- 1 tablespoon caster sugar
- 450g cherries (or 400g frozen cherries)
- 3 tablespoons granulated sugar
- 1 tablespoon cornflour
- 1 lemon
- 2 tarragon sprigs
- 500ml vegetable oil, plus extra for greasing
- 150g icing sugar

Place the strong white bread flour in a large mixing bowl (or the bowl of a free-standing mixer) and whisk in the sea salt. In a jug, mix together the yeast, caster sugar and 250ml of warm water. Leave for a few minutes. Mix the yeast water into the flour, adding a few more tablespoons of water if the dough needs it to come together – it shouldn't be dry. Knead the dough for 8–10 minutes, until smooth and elastic. Alternatively, use the free-standing mixer with a dough hook. Transfer to a clean, lightly oiled bowl and leave to prove for 1 hour.

Preheat your oven to 220°C/fan 200°C/gas mark 7. Destone the cherries (if using fresh), and if using frozen, take them out of the freezer 15 minutes before using. Place the cherries in a roasting tray just big enough to hold them in one layer. Sprinkle over the granulated sugar and cornflour. Halve the lemon and squeeze over most of the juice. Toss everything together then place the tray in the oven and roast for 15–20 minutes (depending on whether using fresh or frozen cherries). They should be slightly caramelised, and the juices surrounding them should be sticky and jammy. Remove from the oven and leave to one side to cool. Once cool, pick the tarragon leaves, finely chop and stir through.

As soon as everything is ready, turn the dough onto a lightly floured worktop and knead. Roll into a long even sausage and cut into 12 equal pieces. Roll each piece of dough into a ball. Take a piece of dough, flatten it into a circle in the palm of your hand about 5mm thick, and place a tablespoon of the roasted cherry mixture in the middle, then fold the dough over, so you have a semi-circle. Seal the edges by gently crimping and pressing them together.

When the pies are all ready, pour enough oil into a large frying or saucepan to come 3cm up the sides. Place on a medium heat. The oil is ready when you put a little dough in there and it starts to bubble and turn golden. Gently lower in three or four pies, and fry for 4–5 minutes. When they are golden brown, turn them over and cook for 2–3 minutes more. Transfer to a tray lined with kitchen paper and continue to fry until all the pies are cooked.

Sift the icing sugar into a mixing bowl and squeeze in enough of the remaining lemon juice until you get a thick, but runny icing (you may need a little water too). After 5 minutes, drizzle over the pies, then serve warm or at room temperature.

Shiamishi: *fried orange-blossom custard pies*

In the Orthodox faith, almost every day of the year is dedicated to a saint or martyr, and every church is named after one of these saints. Greek-Cypriot churches celebrate the days of their saint with a religious service and *panigiri* – a kind of church fete or festival. There are games, coffee, rides and the all-important food stalls. You will find souvla and souvlakia, snack stalls lined with rows of *shoushouko* (grape sweets) and candied nuts, and people frying *loukoumades* (doughnuts) and these little parcels of filo pastry wrapped around a sweet semolina cream. Historically, this was almost exclusively where shiamishi were found. Now, you can get them in many bakeries but, a bit like doughnuts by the seaside, these are treats best eaten fresh and hot. If making your own pastry or deep frying seems like too much hassle, I can tell you these little pies are worth the effort. A crisp shell and fragrant, yielding centre, all under a dusting of cinnamon-sugar... Absolutely worth it.

MAKES 24

1 litre vegetable oil, plus extra for the tray
200g caster sugar
2 pieces of mastic (see page 284), optional
160g fine semolina
1 tablespoon orange blossom water
500g plain flour
½ teaspoon fine sea salt
½ teaspoon baking powder
150ml olive oil
250g icing sugar
2 teaspoons ground cinnamon

Grease a 30 × 25cm baking or roasting tray with a little oil and set to one side. Pour 1.2 litres of water into a saucepan, stir in the caster sugar and place on a medium heat. Grind the mastic with a little extra caster sugar in a pestle and mortar until fine, and add to the pan. When the water is hot, but not boiling, pour the semolina in a slow, steady stream, whisking constantly. Add the orange blossom and keep whisking until it starts to bubble. It should be thick within a few minutes. When it is ready, spoon it into the greased tray and leave it to one side to cool – the custard should be around 1.5cm thick.

While it is cooling, make the dough. Place the flour in a large mixing bowl and whisk in the salt and baking powder. Make a well in the middle and pour in the olive oil. Use your fingers to rub the oil into the flour, then slowly pour in 200ml of tepid water. Bring the dough together, adding more water if necessary – you may need an extra one or two tablespoons. You want the dough to be on the slightly sticky side, rather than too dry. Knead it until smooth, then leave it to rest in a clean bowl, covered with a tea towel, for 30 minutes.

The next bit sounds fiddly but once you get in a rhythm it's not too bad – it's meditative, even. Clear your worktop, have a bowl with olive oil at the ready and grease a large baking tray. Slice the set semolina into 24 squares, so in a grid of four by six. Cut the dough into four, for ease. Take one of the pieces and divide into six small balls. Roll one of the balls into a rough square or circle, around 18cm big, as thin as you can. Then place one of the semolina squares in the middle and fold each side over the semolina, like an envelope. There should be pastry all around the custard square also, like a lip all the way around. Once it is all enclosed, place on a lightly floured tray and keep going until all the pastry and all the semolina is used.

When the shiamishi parcels are all ready, place the oil in a large pan on a medium heat and bring to 160°C. If you put a piece of bread, or even dough, in the oil, you will know it is ready when it starts to sizzle and turn golden. In batches, so as not to overcrowd the pan, gently lower the parcels into the oil and fry for around 3 minutes on each side, until golden all over. Remove with a slotted spoon onto a piece of kitchen paper, then serve immediately, dusted with the icing sugar mixed with the cinnamon. Keep frying until they are all cooked and eat while still hot.

(Photos overleaf)

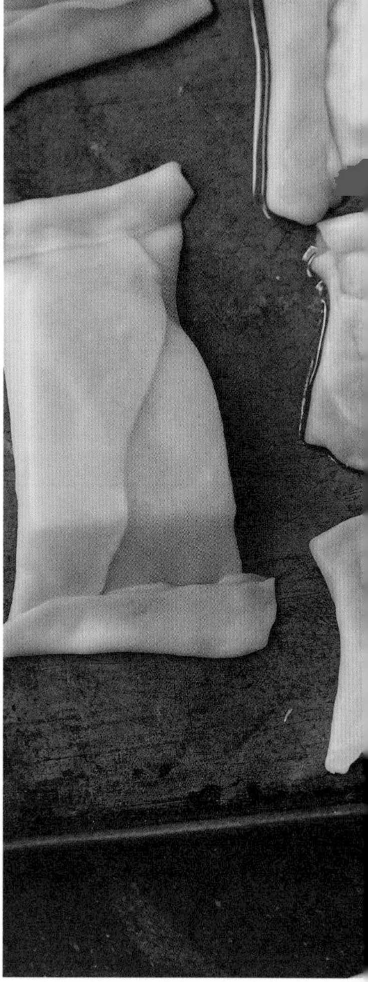

Shiamishi (page 250)

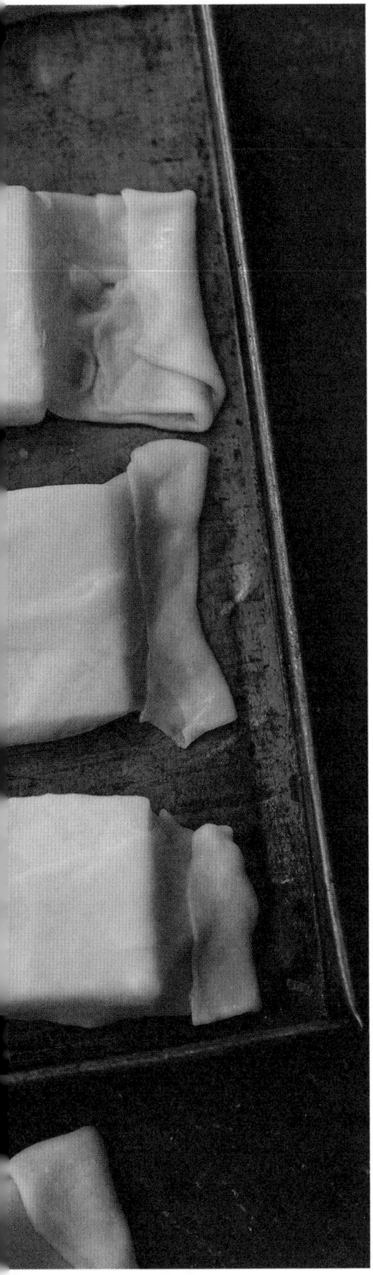

Anoush abour: *Christmas barley pudding, the oldest dessert in the world*

This style of stirred grain pudding appears in various forms throughout different countries and is significant in several religions. In Greece and Cyprus we have koliva (page 46), a memorial food made with wheat berries. In the Middle East, *burbara* is eaten on the feast of St Barbara (4th December), and in Ukraine *kutya* is the pudding of a twelve-course meatless celebration on Christmas Eve. In Turkey it is called *ashure*, and is often made with beans and referred to as 'Noah's pudding', and is eaten during Muharram, the first month of the Islamic calendar. Versions are mentioned in both the Old Testament and the Qur'an.

It is said this is the oldest dessert in the world. After forty days and forty nights on the ark there was little food left, so Noah asked everyone to contribute what ingredients they had and added them to a large pot of boiling water. Slowly he cooked the pudding and as he did the rain stopped and they arrived at the Mountains of Ararat. It was shared among everyone, and for this reason anoush abour is made in large quantities and distributed among friends and neighbours, regardless of their beliefs. It is seen as an offering of peace and a sign of goodwill.

Although it translates as 'sweet soup', this Armenian version is a dessert – slow-cooked, soft and jewelled with sweet fruit. This recipe is based on one that Sharice Babakhani gave me. Her Armenian grandmother, Azadouhi, would always make it for New Year's Day, the creamy grains laced with rose water, subtly sweet and adorned with brightly coloured hundreds and thousands – a touch I particularly love and have adopted.

SERVES 6

250g pearl barley
1 cinnamon stick
150g dried apricots
150g golden raisins
1 teaspoon ground cinnamon
¼ teaspoon ground cloves
½ teaspoon fennel seeds
250g blanched nuts – walnuts, almonds, pistachios and pine nuts
200g honey
1 pomegranate
2 tablespoons rose water
Hundreds and thousands, edible rose petals or candied fennel seeds, optional

Start preparing the day before you want to serve the anoush abour. Place the pearl barley in a large bowl and cover with plenty of cold water. Leave to one side for 2 hours. Drain and place in a large pan with the cinnamon stick and 2.5 litres of water. Bring to the boil over a high heat, then reduce to a low heat, cover and simmer for 1½ hours. Remove from the heat. Leave to one side to cool, adding more water if it has almost completely been absorbed. Boil a kettle. Finely chop the dried apricots and place in a small pan with the raisins and cover with 300ml of just-boiled water. Stir in the ground cinnamon and ground cloves. Lightly crush the fennel seeds and stir them in, too. Cover and leave both pans overnight.

The next day, chop 150g of the mixed nuts and add to the pan with the dried fruit along with the honey. If your fruit has entirely absorbed the liquid, you may want to add a couple of tablespoons of water. Bring to a simmer over a medium heat, then cook for 5–8 minutes, until there is no liquid left in the pan, or only a very reduced amount. Stir into the cooked pearl barley and place the large pan on a low heat to warm through for around 15 minutes. While it is on the hob, pick the pomegranate seeds. When the pudding is ready, stir in the rose water and serve the anoush abour warm, or at room temperature. Garnish with the remaining nuts and pomegranate seeds, and hundreds and thousands or candied fennel seeds, if using.

(Photos overleaf)

Anoush abour (page 254)

6 *Sweet preserves and drinks*

It is hard to write this without sounding hugely biased, but I am told time and again from visitors how astounded they are by the hospitality in Cyprus. I also feel this way about many eastern Mediterranean and Middle Eastern countries and communities – even if someone has very little they will invite you in and give you something to eat. For Greeks and Cypriots glyko is a go-to offering. Preserving fruits, vegetables and nuts in sugar is an age-old technique to make the best of whatever bounty nature is offering, so that all through the year there is something sweet to eat. I have even tried glyko made with olives and tomatoes. This feels particularly relevant during times of fasting; Great Lent in particular can seem long and challenging and a small sweet pick-me-up is often appreciated.

Rose petal jam

While making rose water is relatively technical (see page 285), making rose jam is surprisingly simple. The key is to use heavily perfumed, organic roses. It is the damask rose (*Rosa damascena*), an ancient hybrid, that is most often used for rose water and syrup, thanks to its strong and intoxicating fragrance. And it was the damask rose that we used to make this delicate, pretty jam during a trip to the annual Agros rose festival in Cyprus. Regardless of which rose petals you have, as long they're edible and haven't been exposed to pesticides (see page 290 for stockists), do give this jam a go.

MAKES ABOUT 1.2KG

250g organic edible rose petals (see introduction)
1kg jam sugar
1 lemon
5 tablespoons liquid pectin

Triantaphyllo (rose syrup)

100g organic edible rose petals (see introduction)
500g granulated sugar
1 lemon

Place a saucer or side plate in the freezer and sterilise your jars ready for storing the jam. You can do this by washing the jars thoroughly, then drying out in the oven for 15 minutes at 120°C/fan 100°C/gas mark ½. Once they come out of the oven be careful not to touch the inside or you'll need to repeat the process to make them sterile again.

Gently wash the rose petals and place them in a large, heavy-bottomed saucepan or flameproof casserole. Stir in the jam sugar and 200ml of water. Place on a medium-low heat and stir gently until the sugar has dissolved. Once it is no longer grainy, squeeze in the lemon juice, turn the heat up just a little and cook for around 10 minutes, until it starts to thicken. To test the jam, spoon a tiny bit on to one of the plates from your freezer and push your finger through it. If it starts to wrinkle and crease then the jam is ready. If it stays runny then you need to return the plate to the freezer and cook the jam for a further 5–10 minutes. Keep testing the jam on the cold plate until you get to the desired consistency. Turn off the heat and leave to cool for 10 minutes, then spoon the jam into the sterilised jars and seal. It will keep this way for a few months.

For triantaphyllo: If you want to make triantaphyllo (rose syrup) then simply place the rose petals in 500ml of water and add the granulated sugar. Gently bring to the boil then simmer on a medium heat for 10 minutes. Add the juice of the lemon, and simmer for 5 more minutes. Then cool, strain and transfer to sterilised bottles (see page 287). This will keep for a few months; once opened, store in the fridge.

Roasted apricot compote

Apricot is my all-time favourite jam but the fruit in compote form is equally delicious – and even more versatile. This is perfect with the rice pudding on page 242 (instead of strawberries), the mahalabia on page 238, or as part of a breakfast meze with fresh bread. Heaven.

MAKES ABOUT 1KG

800g apricots
400g granulated sugar
3 tablespoons water
1 lemon
2 tablespoons orange blossom water, optional

Preheat your oven to 180°C/fan 160°C/gas mark 4. Halve the apricots, remove the stones, and cut any large cheeks in half again. Place the fruit in a large roasting tin, and add the granulated sugar and three tablespoons of water. Squeeze in the juice of the lemon and add the orange blossom water, if using. Mix together and leave to one side for 10 minutes. Meanwhile, carefully crack open three of the apricot stones (use a nut cracker if you have one, or place them in a sandwich bag and crack with a rolling pin) and take out the kernel from the centre of the stone. Place the three kernels into the tray, and stir in, then set the tray aside. After 10 minutes, transfer the tray to the oven and bake for 1 hour, stirring every 20 minutes or so, crushing with the back of a fork until the apricots are sticky and cooked down, and just a little golden around the edges. Remember it will thicken as it cools, so don't worry if it is a little on the liquid side at this stage.

If you want to store this for the future, transfer to sterilised jars while still hot, and seal (see page 287). It will now keep for a few months. Otherwise, leave to cool, then transfer to airtight containers and keep in the fridge for a few weeks.

Pumpkin and geranium preserve

A great seasonal preserve to enjoy as a jam or like a Cypriot spoon sweet, served in a small bowl to eat with a teaspoon and a glass of ice-cold water. If you can't find scented geranium leaves, do not despair. Replace them with a few teaspoons of orange blossom or rose water at the end to taste. A cinnamon stick would work well, for a more spiced, wintry finish.

MAKES ABOUT 1.1KG

1kg pumpkin
2 oranges
1 lemon
800g granulated sugar
2 scented geranium leaves

Cut the pumpkin in half and scoop out the seeds. Cut in half again and peel the quarters. If you have a food processor with a coarse grating attachment then use that to grate the flesh. Otherwise finely chop the flesh using a large, sharp knife. Place the pumpkin in a large, heavy-bottomed saucepan. Finely grate in the zest of the oranges and lemon. Squeeze the juice from all the fruit into a measuring jug and top with enough water so you have 300ml. Pour this into the pan and stir in along with the sugar and geranium leaves. Place the pan on a high heat, bring to the boil then reduce the heat to low and simmer for 4–8 minutes until the pumpkin is just tender. The time will depend on whether you grated or finely chopped it; carefully taste a bit to see how it yields – you want it to be turning tender. Turn the heat up to a boil again and cook rapidly for 15–20 minutes, stirring often, until the jam is sticky, glossy and thickened, and the liquid has almost completely reduced. Once it is ready, transfer to sterilised jars (see page 287) and seal while still hot. Alternatively, leave to cool, and store in airtight containers in the fridge for a few weeks.

Date and cardamom butter

Dates are in abundance in Cyprus and the Middle East, and are a popular unprocessed, nutritious, sweet snack. Cooking them down this way turns them into a delicious, *nistisimo* spread – perfect on toast or crackers. You can switch up the spices, but date with cardamom is my favourite pairing.

ENOUGH FOR 8–10 SERVINGS

200g medjool dates
2 oranges
5 cardamom pods
½ teaspoon fine sea salt
Pistachio and edible rose petals, to garnish, optional

Halve the dates, remove and discard the stones and place the fruit in a small saucepan. Squeeze over the juice of both the oranges and top with enough water to just cover the fruit. Bring to the boil over a medium heat. Once boiling, reduce the heat to low and simmer for 20 minutes, until the dates are tender. Meanwhile, remove the seeds from the cardamom pods (discarding the pods), and finely grind using a pestle and mortar. Place the softened dates into a food processor with the crushed cardamom seeds and the salt. Blitz to a smooth paste – add a couple of tablespoons of the cooking liquid to help the paste get going, if needed. If the spread feels a little on the loose side, return the blended mixture back to the pan and cook over a low heat for 5 minutes until thickened and dried out a little. Spoon the paste onto a serving dish and garnish with chopped pistachios and rose petals, if you like.

Sykomaitha: *fig, anise and almond wheel*

On visiting my maternal grandparents' village, my aunty Androulla would (and continues to) fill my pockets with her homemade sykomaitha wheels before I left. It's meant to be eaten alongside an evening drink, or even as part of a meze, but I love eating slivers of it as a snack. This is a traditional way of preserving figs, plentiful throughout the eastern Mediterranean. Over there, the mixture is wrapped in fig leaves and dried in the sun, but slowly baking it in a low oven also does the trick. Made this way, sykomaitha will happily last for months.

MAKES 5 WHEELS

10 fig leaves
250g dried figs
4 tablespoons ouzo, mastiha liqueur or zivania (see pages 285–6)
40g almonds or walnuts
2 fennel herb fronds (if you can get it)
3 black peppercorns
¼ teaspoon aniseed
¼ teaspoon ground cinnamon
1 tablespoon caster sugar, optional
5 tablespoons petimezi (grape molasses) or honey
Olive oil

Soak the fig leaves in a large bowl of cold water. Finely chop the dried figs (discarding the stalk ends) and place in a large bowl. Stir in the ouzo, mastiha liqueur or zivania and leave to one side for 30 minutes. Chop the almonds or walnuts – I like a mixture of very fine and slightly larger pieces. Finely chop the fennel herb, if using. Use a spice mill or pestle and mortar to grind the black peppercorns and aniseed until fine.

Preheat your oven to 140°C/fan 120°C/gas mark 1. When the chopped figs are ready, add the chopped nuts, fennel and all the ground spices to the bowl. Mix together well and knead with your hands until you have a smooth paste. Taste a little bit and if it is a tad bitter, knead in the sugar until well combined.

I find it easier and less messy to make the wheels in conveyor-belt fashion. Lay five of the soaked fig leaves out in front of you. Divide the fig mixture equally into five, roll into balls and place each in the centre of a leaf. Flatten each ball down with the palm of your hand. Brush each fig patty with the grape must or honey, turning over and brushing the other side too, then top with one of the remaining fig leaves. Tuck in the edges of the leaves, and tie each wheel up with string, so that the mixture inside is completely encased. Oil a large baking sheet. Place the wheels on the baking sheet bake for about 2 hours, so that they are golden on the outside and intense and dried out in the middle. When you press on them, they should be firm, not squishy. Leave to cool before serving with cheese or as part of a meze.

If stored in an airtight container in a cool dark place, these sykomaitha will last for months in their leaves.

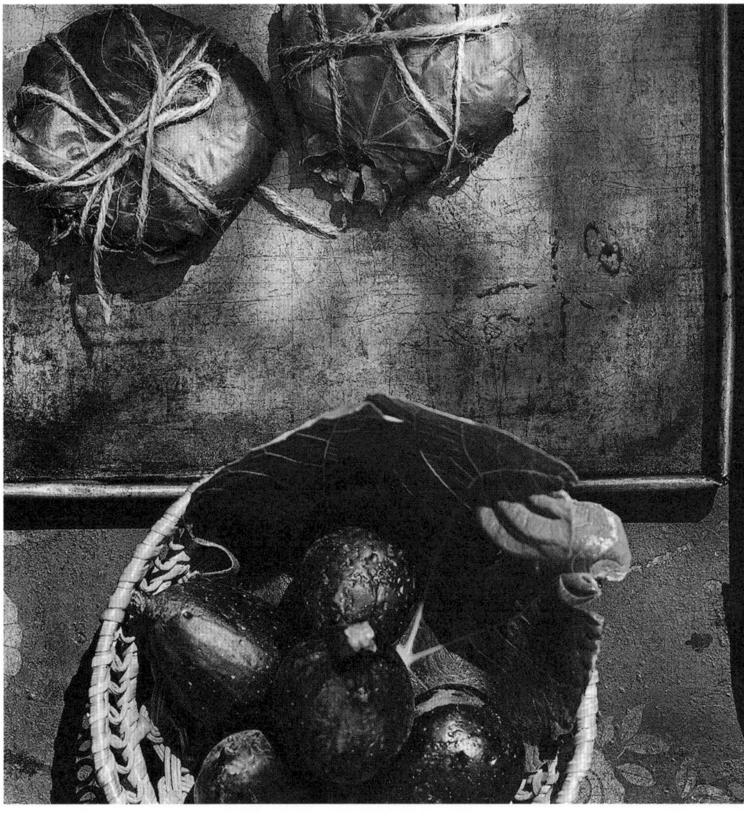

Glyko tou koutaliou: *spoon sweets*

Whether you are visiting the home of a friend, relative or someone you hardly know, the first thing any self-respecting Greek or Cypriot host will offer you is glyko. These are tooth-achingly sweet preserved fruits (or nuts or vegetables) that are served on a small (often glass) plate or bowl, with a fork and glass of ice-cold water. Because of the year-round bounty on Cyprus there is never a shortage of produce to drown in syrup – you'll even find baby aubergines and tomatoes preserved in this way.

Kydoni: *quince*

If you are keen to try your hand at making glyko, kydoni (quince) is a good place to start, as it is probably one of the easiest things to preserve (with karydaki, opposite, being the hardest – I like to give you options). And the flavour is familiar, as preserved quince is much loved in many countries – think membrillo in Spain and quince cheese in the UK.

MAKES ABOUT 3KG

4 lemons
2kg quince
1.4kg granulated sugar
3 scented geranium leaves

You will need some sterilised jars (see page 287). Squeeze one of the lemons into a large pan of water. Peel the quince, cut into quarters and cut out the core. If they are small, leave them this size. If they are extraordinarily large (as some quince are), cut the wedges in half again, placing them in the lemon water as you go to stop them discolouring. When they are all prepared, place the pan on a high heat and bring to the boil. Boil for 20 minutes, then drain the quince and reserve the water. Place 1.2 litres of the cooking water back in the pan with the sugar and scented geranium leaves, and stir together. Squeeze in the juice of the remaining three lemons and bring to the boil over a medium heat. Boil for 15 minutes, then return the poached quince back to the pan. Reduce the heat a little and cook for a further 15–20 minutes, or until the syrup is thick, and the quince is tender. Spoon the hot fruit and syrup into sterilised jars, and seal while hot. Stored this way, placed in a dark cool cupboard, the unopened jars will keep for months.

(Photo overleaf)

Karydaki: *green walnuts*

Green walnuts are one of the most popular glyko, a real delicacy. The method for preserving them is laborious but is thought to showcase good kitchen skills. 'Green' walnuts are young walnuts, still in their green casing before it has time to harden completely and the inside has had time to develop into the nut we are more familiar with. You will often find them stored in jars, pickled or in syrup. Pickling lime is a traditional ingredient, used to retain the crunch and crispness of whatever it is that is being preserved, but if it is hard to find, then you can leave it out.

MAKES ABOUT 30

1kg small, green walnuts
2 tablespoons pickling lime, optional
3 lemons
1kg caster sugar
1 cinnamon stick
6 cloves
2 scented geranium leaves, optional

Start by peeling and soaking the walnuts. Although my yiayia would do this with a paring knife, the easiest way is with a vegetable peeler. Either way, you need to wear gloves or the young walnuts will turn your hands black. You just want to peel off the dark green outer layer, as if peeling a carrot. Slice off the tops where they were attached to the tree, and prick the walnuts all over with the tip of the knife. Place in a large bowl of cold water for eight days, changing the water every day (even twice a day if you can).

Early in the morning on the eighth day (you'll want to start this process as soon as you can), dissolve the lime in a large bowl of cold water and stir in the walnuts. Leave for 4 hours, or until the nuts feel hard. Drain and rinse them under running water to really rinse off the lime (skip this step if you aren't using lime). Place the walnuts in a large pan of fresh water and bring to the boil. Boil for a couple of minutes, drain and repeat this boiling process twice more. On the third boil, reduce the heat and leave the walnuts to cook for 1–1½ hours, or until they are tender. You can check this by piercing a walnut on a skewer or sharp knife and seeing if it slides off. It should fall off easily. When they are ready, remove from the heat, drain and leave to cool.

Place the cooled walnuts in a bowl, cover with cold water and the juice from two of the lemons and leave for 1 hour. Drain the walnuts, then place in a large pan with the caster sugar, cinnamon, cloves, geranium leaves (if using) and just enough water to cover – about a litre. Bring to the boil over a medium-high heat, then reduce the heat a little and rapidly simmer until the syrup coats the back of a spoon. Skim off any scum that rises to the surface while boiling. When it is all ready, squeeze and stir in the juice of the final lemon, then spoon everything into sterilised jars (see page 287). Seal and keep in a cool dark cupboard.

(Photo overleaf)

Ypovrichio: *mastic spoon sweet*

This glyko is also known as a 'submarine', and is my Greek childhood in a jar. We'd walk to the corner *bakali* (greengrocer) and buy a jar for our afternoon sugar fix. At home, we'd take a teaspoon of the thick white paste, then dip it into a glass of iced water to set the sweet a little, then eat it like a lollipop.

Submarine isn't strictly considered a fasting treat, but it is *nistisimo*, and we all deserve something sweet and a bit of fun now and then.

MAKES ABOUT 600ML

500g caster sugar
1 tablespoon lemon juice
½ teaspoon mastic pieces
¼ teaspoon vanilla extract

Sterilise some small jars (see page 287).

Reserve one teaspoon of caster sugar, then place the rest in a heavy-bottomed pan with 300ml of water. Heat gently over a medium heat until the sugar is completely dissolved. Squeeze in half a tablespoon of lemon juice, then turn up the heat a little and bring to the boil. Leave it to bubble away for around 15 minutes until the mixture starts to thicken. To test if the glyko is ready, spoon a little of the thickened syrup into a glass of cold water. Use your fingers to see if it can form a little ball; if it isn't quite at that stage, return the pan to the hob for a further 5 minutes, then try again. When the glyko is ready, place the pan in a sink filled with a couple of inches of cold water, and leave to cool completely.

Meanwhile, grind the mastic in a pestle and mortar with the reserved teaspoon of caster sugar until completely ground. When the glyko is completely cool, add a further half-tablespoon of lemon juice, the ground mastic and the vanilla extract. Beat it vigorously with a wooden spoon until thoroughly integrated, white and glossy. If the paste is a little too thick to beat, loosen it with a splash of water. When the glyko is ready, turn it out on to a clean, damp worktop and knead it until it feels rubbery. Pop the glyko into a sterilised jar, and seal. Unopened, this will keep for months, but once opened store in a cool dark spot or the fridge. Serve the jar of submarine with a glass of iced water. Take a teaspoon, scoop out a little of the glyko and dip into the water. It will help set it a little, like a lollipop. Refreshing, sweet and fun.

Glyko, from left: karydaki (page 271); ypovrichio (page 272); kydoni (page 270)

Russian priests, kvass and a plant-based diet

The importance of kvass for Russian Orthodox priests came to my attention when the food writer Olia Hercules translated some of their fasting literature for me. Kvass is a fermented drink (*kvasit* means 'to ferment') predominantly made from rye bread or grains, and traditionally flavoured with seasonal fruit, herbs and even vegetables. And while some kvass may be slightly alcoholic, the percentage is very low (usually less than 1%). In the late 19th century, it was found to contribute to the digestion of hard-to-digest plant-based foods – hence its popularity with priests and monks who spend more than half the year fasting.

In the past I've found the fermentation process intimidating, however I've also found a plant-based diet to be hard on my digestive system, so I was keen to make kvass while I was writing this book to see if it would act as an aid. I'm pleased to say it has. I am still not the most adventurous fermenter – bread-based kvass seemed beyond my comfort zone – but after researching fruit bases, I felt like that was a good place to start. It is the easiest ferment for beginners, as it can be tasted as it is made, and can be made with an abundance of any sweet, ripe fruit. Once you get going I promise you it is something you won't even think about and can be made with whatever seasonal produce you have around.

MAKES A 1-LITRE JAR

1 tablespoon honey
2g fast-action dried yeast
750ml purified water
A pinch of fine sea salt

And one of the following combinations:

225g raspberries or strawberries, hulled and roughly chopped
2 mint sprigs, leaves picked

Or,

200g rhubarb, sliced
2 thin slices of fresh ginger
1 apple core

Or,

3 pears, sliced
1 tablespoon raisins

Sterilise your jar (see page 287) and place your chosen fruit and flavouring inside. Mix the honey and yeast with a little of the water and add to the jar with the remaining water – you want to fill the jar but leave a 2cm gap between the contents and the lid. Add the salt, seal with the lid, give it a gentle shake to mix everything together then leave to one side. You want to give it a little shake a couple of times a day while it is fermenting.

After one or two days you should start to see the bubbles inside. When you do, release the lid and let out a little of the air. At this point you can leave the kvass for up to one week, depending on what fruits you are using and their sugar content. You are essentially aiming for fruit that looks like it has been poached or cooked with even more bubbles around it. If you are unsure, taste the liquid every day – this is the best way to check when it is ready. When it is to your liking, strain the kvass and discard the fruit. Bottle the kvass and pop it in the fridge – this will stop it fermenting further. However, if you want a more carbonated, fermented kvass, just leave it out of the fridge for a couple more days once it is strained and bottled.

Jallab

This rich, treacly drink – garnished, intriguingly, with nuts and raisins – is popular throughout the Middle East. It is mostly bought as a ready-made cordial to be diluted, and though it can be hard to get hold of in the UK, it is very easy to make. The only missing element is that there is a smoky, incense flavour to the premixed stuff that is difficult to achieve at home. However, it is still utterly delicious without.

SERVES 6

4 tablespoons date molasses
4 tablespoons grape molasses
2 tablespoons pomegranate molasses
2 teaspoons rose water
½ lemon
2 tablespoons pine nuts
2 tablespoons golden raisins

Place the three kinds of molasses in a large jug. Add the rose water and squeeze in the lemon juice, discarding the pips. Top with 1 litre of cold water and stir well. Taste and add a little more water if you like. Decant into ice-filled glasses and garnish each drink with a teaspoon of pine nuts and a teaspoon of golden raisins.

Sharbat: *mint and rose lemonade*

The combination of lemon and mint is popular all over the world, but I love the eastern Mediterranean and Middle Eastern addition of rose water. It's subtle, but elevates this familiar drink to something special.

SERVES 4

4 lemons
4 tablespoons caster sugar
1 tablespoon rose water
3 mint sprigs
2 large handfuls of ice

Finely grate the zest of two lemons (be careful not to get any of the white pith as this will make it bitter) and place in a blender with the juice from all four. Add the sugar, rose water, leaves from the mint sprigs and 350ml of water. Blitz on a high speed until smooth. Divide the ice and remaining mint leaves between four glasses and pour over the sharbat. Serve straight away.

Sbiten, uzvar: *spiced honey drinks*

Sbiten and uzvar are traditional Russian and Ukranian drinks, and are especially delicious in the winter months when you need something sweet to keep you going during a fast. Sbiten is usually served warm and uzvar cool, but to be honest both work perfectly either way. If you think that a shot of something stronger would be a nice addition, you are not wrong. It's not fasting-friendly, but a little vodka or brandy doesn't go amiss for hot toddy vibes.

Sbiten

SERVES 8

150g blackberry jam
150g honey
2 cinnamon sticks
8 cloves
1 teaspoon ground ginger

Place all the ingredients with 1.2 litres of water in a large saucepan and slowly bring to the boil over a medium heat. Boil for 5 minutes, until the blackberry jam and honey have dissolved, then remove from the heat. Leave to cool to room temperature and strain out the spices. Transfer to a clean pan, bring to a simmer and serve hot. Otherwise, transfer to a sterilised bottle (see page 287) and keep in the fridge to warm as needed (or drink cool).

Uzvar

SERVES 8–10

150g dried apple
100g dried pear
50g dried prunes
50g dried cherries (or even dried dark mulberries if you have them)
1 cinnamon stick
Honey, to taste

Place all the dried fruit and the cinnamon stick in a large saucepan and cover with 2.5 litres of cold water. Leave for 1 hour then bring to the boil over a medium heat. Once boiling, reduce the heat to low and simmer for 30 minutes. Remove the pan from the heat, and leave to cool completely (ideally overnight). Once cool, strain the liquid and store in sterilised bottles in the fridge (see page 287). Discard the cinnamon stick and keep the dried fruit to have for breakfast or pudding. Serve the uzvar cold or warm, with honey to sweeten as needed.

Dasogalo: *spiced bread and almond milk*

Hailing from the Greek island of Patmos, dasogalo is essentially a traditional form of almond milk, made creamier and thicker with bread. Traditionally it is made and consumed on Good Friday, using the bread that has been presented in the church and blessed by the priest. It is a lovely creamy drink when you're not drinking dairy – and is surprisingly refreshing.

SERVES 4

225g plain white bread (not sourdough)
100g blanched or ground almonds
2 pieces of mastic, or ½ tablespoon rose water
75g caster sugar
¼ teaspoon ground cinnamon
Nutmeg, to finish

Remove and discard the crust from the bread and chop the rest into small cubes. Place in a large saucepan with the almonds and 1.5 litres of water. Grind the mastic, if using, with a little caster sugar using a pestle and mortar or spice grinder, then add it to the pan with the rest of the caster sugar. Place the pan on a medium heat and gently bring everything to the boil. Reduce the heat and simmer for 5 minutes. Blitz it all up with a stick blender until creamy and very smooth. Strain the mixture through a fine sieve into a jug and chill until needed. If you're using rose water, stir it in now, a little at a time to taste. Serve the dasogalo over ice, finished with a sprinkle of ground cinnamon and fresh grating of nutmeg.

Grapefruit, orange and bergamot cordial

My final piece of research for this book was a visit to the Monastery of Saint Herakleidios in Cyprus, where the nuns specialise in making *nistisimo* preserves and snacks. (All Orthodox monks and nuns adhere to fasting rules, but that's not to say they are all known for their recipes.) For the nuns here, producing *nistisimo* food and drink is one of the main sources of income for the monastery, alongside gold-thread embroidery and icon painting.

There is a simplicity and gentleness to the monastery that induces a sense of tranquillity as soon as you step through the gates, due in part to the gardens that surround the church and ancient relics. As well as plenty of fruit and nut trees, there are acres of olive groves, and beehives from which the nuns harvest honey.

There are forty nuns at St Herakleidios and they make everything from traditional glyko and preserved olives, to more modish praline pastes and cocoa-based sweets. My favourite was the almond spoon-sweet for which they are quite well known. After a walk around the grounds, Sister Theofano brought out a tray with glasses and a jug filled with homegrown, homemade grapefruit and orange cordial. On that especially hot and humid day, it was sheer delight. This recipe is inspired by the nuns' recipe. You'll need around six to eight fruits, depending on their size. I always like to include two or three lemons, especially if I can't get hold of bergamots.

MAKES AROUND 2 LITRES

750g caster sugar
750ml freshly squeezed citrus juice – a couple of grapefruit and bergamot, topped up with orange, works well

Place the caster sugar in a large saucepan and stir in 750ml of cold water. Pop on a medium heat and stir until the sugar has dissolved. Turn the heat up and bring to the boil, then reduce a little, just so that the mixture maintains a steady rolling boil without overflowing. Cook for 8 minutes, until syrupy but not golden or coloured at all. Pour the citrus juice into the pan, through a coarse sieve to catch any pips, and stir to combine. Reduce to a medium heat and simmer for 4–5 minutes. I don't like to bring my cordial to the boil; I just heat it through enough to combine it well but not kill off all the vitamins. However, you will end up with a more concentrated cordial if you let it simmer, which is not a bad thing. Spoon off any scum that has risen to the surface, then leave the cordial to cool slightly. Meanwhile sterilise glass bottles and lids (see page 287), as this will preserve your cordial for longer – you'll be able to keep it unopened for months in the fridge. Use a funnel to pour the slightly cooled cordial into the bottles, then seal and leave to cool completely. Store in the fridge, then serve topped with ice and cold still or sparkling water for a refreshing drink.

A short guide to my essential pantry

The majority of ingredients in this book will be familiar and accessible – most are stocked in large supermarkets or online. However, due to the variety of cuisines contained within, some more unusual items may need explanation or hunting down. Here is a glossary of sorts, and a suppliers list (page 290) might help you fill in any gaps.

• **Aniseed:** A little harder to find than most spices, aniseed is commonplace in eastern Mediterranean, Middle Eastern and north African cooking. These little seeds have a liquorice, anise flavour and are the basis of the famous Greek spirit ouzo. Although aniseeds look and taste a little like fennel seeds, do try to hunt them out. For recipes like the koulouri (page 35), they are a key flavour and substitutions just won't do.

• **Baharat:** The Arabic word for 'spices', this is a blend used throughout Middle Eastern cooking (much like garam masala in India). Different regions and households will have different mixtures, used in extensively in home cooking. You can buy it pre-blended or make your own (see the recipe on page 110).

• **Carob, carob molasses, carob syrup:** Nicknamed 'the black gold of Cyprus', carob was Cyprus's biggest export for centuries. A legume, native to the Mediterranean, carob pods are black and grow on evergreen trees. When ripe, the pods contain a sweet pulp that is either made into molasses or dried, roasted and ground into a powder. Naturally sweet, dark and nutty, it is often likened to chocolate and used as a healthier alternative (as unlike cocoa, it doesn't need to be sweetened).

• **Dried mint:** Used widely in Cyprus, dried mint is one of the most prominent flavours in our cooking. You can buy it, but mint is easy to grow and even easier to dry. Just hang (washed and dried) sprigs upside down in a dark but warm spot. Then, after a few weeks you'll see the leaves have become crisp. Simply take a few leaves in the palm of your hand and crush them into your food as needed.

• **Dukkah:** A blend of spices and nuts that is used to garnish and finish dishes all over Egypt and the Middle East, and very simple to make (see page 108 for my recipe).

- **Extra virgin olive oil:** Or as we say *kalo lathi* – good oil. Be sure to invest in the best quality extra virgin olive oil you can afford. Don't use your good oil for cooking, it's a waste, but be sure to dress salads, mezethes and stews with a drizzle or two for a beautiful finish. If you want to be super savvy (for price, and quality), buy it in a large oil drum from any good Greek grocer.

- **Fava beans:** Dried broad beans are not as commonly found as chickpeas, but are easily purchased online or from specialist shops.

- **Filo pastry:** While you may be familiar with the filo pastry sold in large supermarkets, there are in fact lots of types. Filo means 'leaf' in Greek, and refers to the thickness (or in this case thinness) of the pastry. Homemade village-style filo (as found on page 250) is rolled out with a long wooden dowel, and often used for pies such as spanakopita. Commercial filos – those extra thin sheets – are used for things like baklava and sweet syrupy puddings.

- **Fine bulgur wheat:** Exactly what it says on the tin, a finer grain of the regular bulgur wheat. Fine bulgur is usually only found in Greek, Turkish and Middle Eastern shops. However, it can be easily bought online, or you can make your own by blitzing regular bulgur in a food processor or spice grinder until the grains have halved in size.

- **Kataifi:** You might recognise this dairy-free pastry that is used throughout Greece, Cyprus and the Middle East – it looks like vermicelli or even Shredded Wheat cereal. It is often referred to as shredded filo pastry, as both are made from just flour, water and oil. However, filo pastry is rolled, whereas kataifi is spun to give it its fine texture.

- **Kolokassi, aka taro:** *Colocasia esculenta* is a winter root vegetable, that's sometimes called elephant ears, thanks to its distinct foliage. It is eaten from Cyprus to Egypt, South East Asia and Hawaii (to name just a few places) often in a stew or soup. There's a knack to preparing it, detailed on page 143.

- **Mastiha, mastic:** An aromatic resin from the Greek island of Chios, mastic is used when ground, however for the best flavour look for it sold as small crystals. To grind it yourself, it must be pounded using a pestle and mortar with a touch of sugar or flour, as it is sticky. Delicious as it is, employ a delicate touch, as too much will make your food bitter.
(Pictured on page 283)

- **Mastiha liqueur:** A sweet Greek liqueur made by distilling mastic (see opposite). Usually served straight up, chilled, after a meal.

- **Mehlepi, mahlab:** The seeds of the St Lucie cherry are ground and used to flavour breads and cake. Similar to mastic, mehlepi can be bought ground but is best bought whole and ground at home as it is needed. Also like mastic, it should be used sparingly.

- **Niseste:** This Greek very fine cornflour (starch) is used to make milk and water puddings, such as my favourite mahalepi (page 238). If you can't get hold of it, it is easily swapped with cornflour.

- **Orange blossom and rose waters:** These scented floral waters are made by boiling the blossom from the bitter orange tree, or rose petals, then condensing the steam in a still or alembic. Fragrant and delicate, the strength of the water varies from brand to brand. I've even come across some in supermarkets that claim to be rose water but are in fact an extract (a stronger product, based on alcohol). Use with caution, and always smell and taste your flower waters before adding to your food.

- **Ouzo:** The most famous Greek spirit, ouzo is an anise flavoured aperitif, not unlike pastis or sambuca.

- **Petimezi, grape must, grape molasses:** Made from boiling down grape juice until thick and syrupy, this is mostly used in baking, and was used as a sweetener before refined sugar became widely available.

- **Pomegranate molasses:** The reduced juice of sour pomegranates is a thick, deep red syrup that has a wonderful sweet and sour taste. It's often used in marinades or for finishing dishes, and is delicious drizzled over salads.

- **Potatoes, Cyprus:** Cyprus potatoes, often sold still with a heavy dusting of the red soil in which they are grown, are much loved for their a distinctive flavour and waxy texture. They are thin skinned, and their yellow flesh has a naturally buttery taste. They're perfect for boiling and using in salads – for maximum flavour, boil them in their skins then peel after they're cooked. They also make excellent chips and roast potatoes.

- **Pul biber:** This dried red pepper is used throughout the Middle East and the eastern Mediterranean. Also known as Aleppo pepper, it isn't as spicy as conventional chilli flakes, but fruity and warm.

- **Sumac:** A coarse powder, burgundy in colour, that looks perhaps like chilli but is in fact ground sumac berries – not at all spicy. Sumac has a delicate acidity, and is often added to recipes at the end of cooking, in the same way you would use lemon juice or zest.

- **Sweet paprika:** In this book, unless I refer to smoked paprika, I am referring to sweet paprika from Serbia or Hungary that is usually unsmoked, unlike the more commonly found Spanish paprika.

- **Tahini:** This paste made from ground sesame seeds is used in everything from dressings and dips, to cakes. In the jar, it will separate into oil and solids, so it needs to be stirred before using.

- **Biber salçasi, Turkish pepper paste:** Think of it like tomato purée, but made with cooked red peppers. Often used as a base for stews, it's a useful addition to any cupboard.

- **Triantaphyllo:** A lurid pink rose flavoured syrup that is drunk as a cordial (with either water or milk) and used as a topping for puddings such as mahalepi (page 238).

- **Vine leaves:** Unless you have your own grapevine, or live near a Greek, Turkish or Middle Eastern grocer, fresh vine leaves might be hard to purchase. You have two options: first, buy them in brine, which you can do in larger supermarkets, speciality shops and online. You must blanch or soak brined leaves first to remove the excess salt. The other option takes more time initially to get going, but is really simple and rewarding: grow your own. We always have bags of vine leaves in the freezer after raiding friends' vines, stocking up for the colder months.

- **Za'atar:** This can refer to either the blend of herbs and spices (see page 111 for a recipe) or a herb of the same name, found in the Middle East, that is very similar to wild thyme.

- **Zivania:** This Cypriot alcoholic drink is made from the grapes and stems left over from the wine season. These are distilled along with local wines to produce a potent spirit that is served ice cold and taken slowly after meals. Most Cypriot households will have a bottle, not just to drink but for medical purposes also. It is rubbed on chests to fight off colds, massaged into aching joints, and is sometimes employed to numb toothache and to help sterilise cuts and wounds.

How to...

How to peel tomatoes: Peel ripe tomatoes easily by cutting a small cross, only 1-2cm each way, at the end of the tomato and place in a large heatproof bowl. Cover the tomatoes with boiling water and leave for a minute or two. Drain away the water when the peel from the cut ends starts to curl away. Then you will be able to easily peel away the skins, using the cut as a starting point. Another way is to grate the tomatoes. This is a little messier, but if you have a coarse handheld grater it isn't too bad. By grating a ripe tomato, you naturally separate the flesh and seeds from the skin, which you then discard. Both methods work in my recipes.

How to prep potatoes, artichokes, quinces and apples: Potatoes can start to discolour when you're peeling and chopping them, especially if you're cooking for a celebration or large family. Half-fill a large bowl with cold water and add a halved lemon. Pop the prepped vegetables in the acidulated water as you go and they won't discolour. You can also do this ahead of time, leaving them in the water for a couple of hours before using them. The same applies to artichokes, quinces and apples, which are even quicker to turn brown.

How to sterilise jars: There are a few ways to do this. I like to wash mine with hot soapy water and give them a good rinse. I then place them upside down on an oven tray with a rack, the lids alongside, and place in a preheated oven (120°C/fan 100°C/gas mark ½) for 15 minutes.

How to make bread dough: When it came to recipe testing this book it became apparent that there was a vast difference to how much water was needed depending on whether the dough was kneaded by hand or with a free-standing mixer. Dough made with 500g of strong bread flour can use anything from 230ml–325ml of warm water – using a mixer will require the higher amount. I have assumed most people will make bread by hand, so have been conservative with measurements. However, try and keep the dough as moist as possible. The more it is kneaded, the more the gluten is built up and the drier the dough becomes. Even after resting the dough, it will be less moist. If you are using a free-standing mixer, then you should feel comfortable to add about 50ml more water than the recipes suggests.

A few thoughts about chickpeas

Actually, I have many thoughts about chickpeas. Firstly, I truly believe if you are making a chickpea recipe, it will more delicious if you use good-quality dried chickpeas. However, for time and other reasons, this isn't always possible, and honestly jarred and tinned chickpeas are very useful and also delicious. I prefer jarred, and you can get lovely ones pretty cheaply in international or specialist food shops, but good-quality, organic tinned ones are also nice. I make a lot of chickpea recipes, and often use them as a base for salads and stews, combined with whatever I have in the fridge and cupboard. Here's how I prepare them.

The measurements

The general rule of thumb is that chickpeas double their weight once cooked – depending on the chickpeas, they can increase by up to two and a half times. So, if a recipe calls for 200g of dried chickpeas, and you want to use jarred or tinned ones then you will need the drained weight of those chickpeas to be 400–500g. Thinking about it the other way, if a recipe calls for 500g of cooked chickpeas, you should start with 250g of dried chickpeas.

Soaking dried chickpeas

To prepare dried chickpeas ready for cooking, you will need to soak them overnight, for at least 12 hours and for up to 24 hours. Place them in a large bowl and cover with plenty of cold water. If your recipe calls for using the cooking liquid, then stir 1 teaspoon of bicarbonate of soda into the soaking water (see why below). If you do not need to keep the cooking water for later on, then just use lots of water. Loosely cover the bowl with cling film and leave to one side.

The secret ingredient

Depending on what you are using your chickpeas for, bicarbonate of soda is a key ingredient to make them more tender and help their skins come off. But when to add the bicarb will change depending on what you are making with the chickpeas. If I am making houmous, I like to keep some of the cooking liquid back to add into the houmous, which makes it light and moussey. In this instance, I wouldn't add bicarbonate of soda to the cooking water. It will not taste good. If, however, I was cooking the chickpeas to add to a soup or stew, where none of the cooking liquid is required, then adding bicarbonate of soda to the saucepan while cooking will help soften them, and will also make peeling them easier.

Cooking chickpeas

When your chickpeas have soaked, drain them in a colander, rinse them well and transfer to a large saucepan. If you haven't used bicarbonate of soda in the soaking process, and your recipe does not require you to reserve and use any cooking water, stir a teaspoon of bicarbonate of soda directly into the chickpeas when they are in the pan, coating them all. Turn on the hob to medium, fry the chickpeas for a couple of minutes, then add enough cold water to cover them by 5cm. If you added bicarbonate of soda during soaking, skip the frying step and just cover the chickpeas with the water. Turn up the heat and bring to the boil, then reduce the heat and simmer for 1–1½ hours until the chickpeas are tender. You may find that some of the skins slip off while cooking and rise to the surface; simply skim these off as they cook.

Peeling chickpeas

If your chickpeas had bicarbonate of soda in the cooking water, the skins should have slipped off and you'll have skimmed them away. If they haven't, drain the cooked chickpeas (keep that cooking liquor to one side) and return them to the pan. Cover the chickpeas in plenty of fresh cold water and place the pan in the sink. Pick up a handful of the chickpeas and rub them between the palms of your hands; as you do so, the skins should come away and fall into the pan, floating to the surface. Transfer the skinned chickpeas to a bowl, skim the fallen skins away and carry on with the rest of chickpeas in the pan.

Why the hassle to peel the chickpeas? The outside is a little waxy and can be tough. When making houmous, it is the skins that give it a grainy texture, which is not what you want (well, it's not what I want). If they don't bother you, then don't worry, but I think this little extra step gives a much smoother, creamier finish to the dish and is well worth doing.

Shops and suppliers

I've tried to write, develop and create recipes that are accessible and easy to recreate at home. Although the majority of ingredients are readily available in most supermarkets, naturally there are a few unusual or harder-to-find items. Where this is the case, I try to give alternatives and options. However if you do want to go the distance, then these are the suppliers to help you out.

Belazu

Belazu specialise in Mediterranean and Middle Eastern ingredients, and can be found in most larger supermarkets. However, you can also order directly from them. I especially love their harissa, spice pastes and balsamic vinegar.

belazu.com/shop

Maddocks Farm

I order scented roses from Maddocks Farm during the summer months to make rose syrup and rose jam (page 263); their fragrance and flavour are heavenly.

maddocksfarmorganics.co.uk

Maltby and Greek

Stockists of classic Greek ingredients and well-known Greek brands. If you want proper Santorini yellow split peas for fava or are struggling to track down kataifi pastry, these are your guys.

Arch 17, Apollo Business Park, Lucey Way, London SE16 4ET; maltbyandgreek.com

Odysea

Traditional Mediterranean products, with a specialism in Greek items. Their various fruit molasses are my go-to, as are their honey, olives, extra virgin olive oil... Everything they import is top notch.

odysea.com

Rooted Spices

Well-sourced, single estate spices as well as their own interesting blends. You can find ingredients such as pul biber or mehlebi/mahleb here. As well as proper sweet, intense cinnamon bark.

rootedspices.com

Sous Chef

An online gourmet haven, Sous Chef stocks hard-to-find pantry ingredients (and equipment) from all over the world. I start by looking for one or two things and never check out without a basket full of treats.
souschef.co.uk

MY LOCAL HEROES

The north London area I live in feels like an epicentre for the Cypriot community, and therefore has lots of great shops. There are a few gems that really deserve to be included (two of which do online ordering).

Deli on the Green

A true family business, run by some of the kindest women I know, Deli on the Green is my go-to place when I just cannot cook any more. Erene is a magnificent cook and two of her recipes feature in this book for you to make at home. Alternatively, you can visit and eat her food here, as well as stocking up on a few select Cypriot products.
251 Hoppers Road, London N21 3NP; 020 8882 5631

Despina Foods

A trip to Despina feels like a fleeting trip to Cyprus. It is always heaving in seasonal produce – including harder-to-find fruit and vegetables. Plus all the Greek Cypriot larder items you could need. And then there is the added bonus of the hot koupes and bourekia that are cooked constantly during the day, left casually on the side for you to help yourself to. Lethal.
456–458 Bowes Road, London N11 1NL; despina-foods.co.uk

Yasar Halim

Turkish Cypriot institution, there are three branches of Yasar Halim, all large and all specialise in baked goods. Expect olive counters, fragrant fresh produce and even barbecue equipment.
yasarhalim.com

Index

A

B

C

D

K

L

M

N

O

P

Q

R

S

T

U

V

W

Y

Z

Exit
Exit

Thank yous

Rowan Yapp, for believing in me from day one and letting me follow you on your journey. Felicity Blunt for always having my back and being a brilliant cheerleader. Lena Hall, for your advice, dedication and care. Thank you for loving *Nistisima* as much as I do. Ellen Williams and Don Shanahan, for shouting about the book and helping get it out in the world, thank you for holding my hand. To Sally Somers, for your care and thoroughness with my words. Vanessa Fogarty for believing in me more than I believe in myself. Rosie Pierce, Joel Arcanjo and Albie Herd, for your help along the way.

Kristin Perers, for taking the most evocative and poetic photographs, and fully immersing yourself in my world. You truly are one of the family; the garage studio always awaits. Tab Hawkins, not only is your vision and style incomparable, your energy is too! It is always like being in Greece and Cyprus when you are here, you create the most immersive worlds. Joss Herd, for bringing my recipes to life. I felt nervous handing them over, but there was no need, you are an artist and a magician. Hattie, for your thoroughness, kindness and being my girl's best pal. Anna Green, for casting your magic wand over all our work and bringing it together so harmoniously and effortlessly.

Huge thanks to Jamie Oliver, Claudia Roden and Itamar Srulovich for your kind words and time – knowing you like the book means the world to me. Nicola Miller, for being one of the first people I reached out to when I started researching many years ago and coming back with a plethora of suggestions on where to start. To the Guild of Food Writers, for awarding me a bursary to aid with my research, enabling me to speak to more people, including some of the monks and nuns who feature in the book.

My right hand woman, Holly O'Neill, I don't know what I would do without you. Not only are you a true friend, you have edited the book with a bluntness I admire enormously, helped me test with a fine-toothed comb when my arms were filled with babies, triple-checked facts when I felt like I was losing the plot, and more than anything you care. I will never be able to thank you enough.

To all the brilliant contributors – I hope I have done your stories and recipes justice. For Sharice Babakhani and Azadouhi Utudjian. Sharice, thank you for sharing your grandmother's recipes with us. I am so glad

Azadouhi knew that we did this; she sounded like a formidable woman. Kristina Vučinić, your biscuits are now one of my favourite fasting treats! I wish we could have included those fantastic photos of your grandma somewhere; I dream of helping her on her tomato preserving days. Elham Matalka, I am so pleased that Lena introduced us. I loved your video calls from Jordan, hearing about all the food you were making and hope to be able to join you one day making maamoul.

Margarita Flouri, Suat Inan, Angeliki Dimaki, Maria Repanos, Amirah Sami – thank you all for your wonderful recipes and stories, and bearing with me and my stream of questions and sporadic emails. Alissa Timoshkina, Olia Hercules and Irina Georgescu, you were all so generous with your time, sharing your recipes and knowledge with me. Erene Panteli – and all the deli ladies – your faith and kindness is inspiring. Without a doubt you are one of the best cooks I know.

Father Augustine, I hope I can visit you one day in Lebanon. I have loved speaking with you and am indebted to Franco Tzouvanni for introducing us. Thank you, Franco! Father John and Dimos from St Demetrios, I appreciate how chaotic it must have been letting us shoot in your church on Easter Saturday and I will forever be grateful to you both for letting it happen. And obviously to my yiayia Martha: my constant inspiration and muse, a fountain of knowledge and the biggest and best critic I know.

To all my friends, especially Lucy Jarrett-Smith and Scott Edwards, Vicke Morrison and Ed O'Brien, Sarah Angell and Ewan Warburton, Carly Peters and Esub Miah, thank you for testing my recipes and your honest feedback! To Claire Cain and Laura McKendry for help with childcare and always having my back.

My family – my mum, dad, sister, yiayia, bapou, Lala, Cassie and Stephen, Carl and Heather – I don't know how I would have got through the last few years without you all. You kept me sane, held the babies and looked after us, with nothing but patience and love. Finally, my biggest champion, Pete. Thank you for hot coffee, taking the morning brunt of the chaos and always putting up with me – I know it's not been easy. You are amazing. And my babies for spurring me on and keeping me on my toes. I love you all.
x

ABOUT THE AUTHOR

Georgina Hayden is a cook, food writer and stylist from north London. She writes for publications such as *The Telegraph*, *Delicious Magazine* and *Observer Food Monthly*, and in 2021 she won the Fortnum & Mason Best Cookery Writer Award for her work in *Waitrose Food* magazine. She has appeared on Radio 4's *Woman's Hour*, and regularly appears on Channel 4's *Sunday Brunch* and BBC1's *Saturday Kitchen*.

Growing up above her grandparents' Greek Cypriot taverna, Georgina developed a love of cooking and storytelling through the recipes passed down to her. She started her career as food assistant, working at various food magazines, and then went on to join Jamie Oliver's food team where she worked for 12 years. Her first book, *Stirring Slowly*, was published in 2016, followed by the book about the food of her Cypriot family, *Taverna*, in 2019. *Nistisima* is her third book.

Georgina documents her recipes and food travels on her Instagram page: **@georgiepuddingnpie**.

REECE · CY
NIA · SLOVAK
YPT · SYRIA ·
BANON · ARM
RUSSIA · UKR
· CYPRUS ·
VAKIA · SERB